It's
Your
Money

It's Your Money

How banking went rogue, where it is now and how to *protect* and *grow* your money

Alan Kohler

NERO

Published by Nero,
an imprint of Schwartz Publishing Pty Ltd
Level 1, 221 Drummond Street
Carlton VIC 3053, Australia
enquiries@blackincbooks.com
www.nerobooks.com

9781760641016 (paperback)
9781743820742 (ebook)

A catalogue record for this
book is available from the
NATIONAL
LIBRARY National Library of Australia
OF AUSTRALIA

Cover design by Ella Egidy
Text design and typesetting by Duncan Blachford

NOTE TO READERS

This publication contains the opinions and ideas of its author. It is sold with the
understanding that neither the author nor the publisher is engaged in rendering
legal, tax, investment, insurance, financial, accounting, or other professional advice
or services. If the reader requires such advice or services, a competent professional
should be consulted. Relevant laws vary from state to state. The strategies outlined
in this book may not be suitable for every individual, and are not guaranteed or
warranted to produce any particular results.

No warranty is made with respect to the accuracy or completeness of the information
contained herein, and both the author and publisher specifically disclaim any
responsibility for any liability, loss or risk, personal or otherwise, which is incurred
as a consequence, directly or indirectly, of the use and application of any of the
contents of this book.

Contents

Introduction

M Y GOAL IN WRITING *IT'S YOUR MONEY* IS threefold. First, to explain, as I see it, what went wrong with a system that was meant to serve you. Second, to unpack why the royal commission's conclusions missed the mark – although the hearings did not. And third – and most importantly – to help you take back control of your finances.

That doesn't necessarily mean doing it yourself. For most people that's either not really possible or not a good idea. It means having enough knowledge and confidence to be a strong customer of the financial services industry.

You are probably already a confident customer of other industries that serve you – from health services to car repairs. Finance and investing may seem more daunting – many people turn to jelly when they have to confront them – but actually the businesses engaged in this industry are just like any others. It's just that they've often exploited a knowledge gap among consumers to their own benefit.

You can put a stop to that now – and this book will show you how.

1

HOW THE
ROT SET IN

I START FROM THE PROPOSITION THAT MOST PEOPLE have good intentions. They don't need rules to make them do the right thing. Laws and regulations are necessary only for the few people who are bad or desperate or greedy enough to harm others. That applies to banking and finance as much as it does to anything else.

Having covered the banking and finance sector – all businesses, in fact – as a journalist for more than forty-five years, I have a clear view of what led to the mess the banks are in today, and how they became corporate pariahs. I don't think it's because bankers or financial advisers are inherently worse people than anyone else. It's more that there's been a failure to regulate them properly, and especially a failure to limit their power and punish transgressions. There are clear limits and consequences in other fields of life, but not in finance. I'm sure there is about the same proportion of people prepared to cut corners and hurt others in banking as there is in the world more generally – the problem is that they've not been reined in.

Sure, along the way there have been a few notably gross offenders who were held to account. There were also some significant individuals who made a positive difference to how the system works. But my contention is that the failures in banking and financial services exposed by the Royal Commission into Misconduct in the Banking, Superannuation and Financial Services Industry (the Hayne Royal Commission), the terrible behaviour, greed and corruption, are mostly due to failures of policy and regulation that allowed them. So let's look at how it all went wrong with the bankers and money managers, and what lessons we can learn from that as their customers.

1

The Banks

THREE SEPARATE EVENTS IN 1992 SOWED THE seeds of Australia's banking crisis. Each of the events had profound unintended consequences for the nation's financial system. It was a big year, beginning with Yeltsin and Bush declaring the end of the Cold War, and ending with Bill Clinton winning the US presidential election. In between, Deng Xiaoping kicked off market reforms in China, the European Union was founded with the signing of the Maastricht Treaty, and Sidney Nolan and Brett Whiteley both died. It was a momentous year for me, too. I turned forty and was appointed editor of *The Age*. The end of the Cold War and Deng's reforms were historic developments, that's for sure, but the three important events for Australian banking that happened in 1992 were as follows. First, the charismatic Peter Smedley, a career executive with the Shell Oil Company, took the reins as CEO of a stuffy old life insurance and wealth management business in Melbourne called Colonial Mutual. Second, Paul Keating created the nation's modern, compulsory superannuation system. And finally, desperate Westpac chairman John Uhrig approached an American named Bob Joss to be CEO, and paid him the earth.

The bancassurance bug

Let's start with Peter Smedley. At the time, Colonial Mutual wasn't a bank and had nothing to do with banking: it had been founded in 1873, as a customer-owned mutual life insurance provider, by Sir Redmond Barry, one of the Victorian colony's leading figures. (Among other things, Barry was the presiding judge at the trial of Ned Kelly. Famously, as he sentenced the bushranger to hang, he said, 'May God have mercy on your soul.') Smedley had a thirty-year career with Shell, travelling around the world and rising through the ranks until he was seen as a contender for the top job. But at the age of forty-nine he had a midlife epiphany. He returned to Australia and got a job as CEO of one of Australia's longest-running, most venerable and conservative life insurance offices.

Smedley was a man in a hurry. An interloper in an unfamiliar world, he needed to prove himself, and he did so with amazing chutzpah. He quickly transformed Colonial from a mutual society into a listed company, and turned it into one of the most rapacious corporate acquirers the Australian stock exchange had ever seen. He made seventeen acquisitions in eight years, earning himself the nickname 'Pacman'. As an editor and then a columnist, I remember being in awe of the man's tireless ambition. I wrote about his rapid-fire takeovers almost as enthusiastically as he made them. Like Paul Keating, Peter Smedley made great copy.

In 1994, Smedley was ahead of his time. He was an early advocate and global pioneer of the return of financial conglomerates, which had been out of favour since the Great Depression gave them a bad name sixty years earlier. In 1933, a landmark piece of US legislation – the Glass Steagall Act – banned trading banks from combining with investment banks and insurance companies. That rule more or less applied around the world, until a new trend changed everything. Smedley introduced Australia to the old but freshened-up concept of 'bancassurance': combining banks with insurance businesses (particularly life insurance businesses, which in those days encompassed pension funds management) with the idea of selling multiple financial products to bank customers.

More importantly, Smedley put bancassurance into practice, by absorbing the State Bank of NSW into the 121-year-old Colonial. (The 'Mutual' had been dropped by then.) In Australia and overseas, this trend had big impacts. In 1998, America's Citibank acquired the insurance company Travelers and, with the backing of Federal Reserve Board chairman Alan Greenspan, forced the repeal of Glass Steagall in 1999. (Many people believe, rightly in my view, that the excesses that resulted from allowing trading banks to move into investment banking led to the 2007–08 global financial crisis.) Executive salaries weren't disclosed in those days, but as Smedley's company grew, his personal wealth would have, too, which must have added to the thrill of the chase. But more on salaries later.

Meanwhile, the Labor government had started privatising the Commonwealth Bank, three decades after the Reserve Bank of Australia was set up in 1960. No longer Australia's central bank, the Commonwealth Bank was simply a government-owned savings and trading bank, and in the wave of privatisations during the 1980s and '90s it was naturally privatised, along with Qantas, CSL (the old Commonwealth Serum Laboratories) and the Victorian electricity industry. The third and final piece of the federal government's stake in the Commonwealth Bank was sold in 1996 for $5 billion, making the total proceeds a bit less than $8 billion.

The first chief executive of the bank once it was publicly listed was David Murray, who had started as a teller in 1966. In the first few years after the float, Murray was focused on settling the business into private ownership. But he soon caught the bancassurance bug, not to mention the takeover bug, and in 2000 Murray's Commonwealth Bank took over Peter Smedley's creation, Colonial, which by then included not just the State Bank of NSW but also a big wealth management and superannuation business called First State.

That sparked a flurry of banks acquiring life insurance and wealth management businesses: NAB acquired MLC, Westpac bought BT Australia, and ANZ went into partnership with the Dutch company ING. Two years earlier, in 2000, Australia's oldest and largest life insurance company, AMP, demutualised, following Colonial's example. It also launched its own bank, AMP Bank. Around the same time, AMP's largest competitor, National Mutual, was taken over by the French life insurer AXA. All of these corporate manoeuvrings had two big effects. They helped enrich the men who ran them, and they blurred the line between banking and investing. In fact, the line was smashed.

As an aside, it's worth noting that a lot of the people in charge of banks in those days – and still some today – were on 'defined benefit' superannuation packages, as opposed to the 'defined contribution' schemes most of us have. For people in defined contribution schemes, what you get out at the end depends on how much you've put in, how well the super fund has done, and whether the markets have been kind to you. With most defined benefit schemes, however, there aren't any actual contributions, and the retirement sum is a percentage of your final salary. The higher the final salary, the higher the benefit. So a CEO who manages to get their salary up by making lots of takeovers, and squeezing out a good short-term profit, can retire on a very nice lump-sum pension indeed. When David Murray 'retired' at the age of fifty-six in 2005, for example, his retirement benefit was $8.8 million.

Anyway, some twenty years after the line between wealth management and banking was blurred and then smashed, it is now being redrawn. The Commonwealth Bank has announced that Colonial is to be 'demerged', having already sold the life insurance division, CommInsure. NAB is demerging MLC. And ANZ has sold the old ING insurance business, now called OnePath, to IOOF. Only Westpac is sticking with its insurance and wealth management acquisition, BT – for the moment, at least. Bancassurance was a twenty-year experiment that didn't work. Not only did the idea of selling more stuff to the same people fail to produce more revenue for less cost, but the takeovers helped destroy the banks' cultures.

Sure, all those mergers made the banks – and their executives' pay packets – much larger, but what the oilman Smedley didn't understand, and what Murray and the others should have understood but probably didn't care about, was that banking and insurance, or wealth management, are fundamentally different businesses. Almost as different as, say, managing a hospital and selling cars. The only things they have in common are that they deal in money and their customers are human beings. Banking is mostly about the management of risk. It has traditionally involved rationing credit, not selling it. Wealth management and insurance are products that have to be sold, and the risks that need to be managed are entirely different. Instead of credit risk, wealth managers and life insurance underwriters have to manage investment risk and 'longevity risk' – the danger that someone will outlive their ability to fund a comfortable retirement.

So, while those mergers weren't disastrous for the executives of the time, who have all moved on to a comfortable retirement or semi-retirement, they were certainly disastrous for future generations of executives and directors – and, of course, for customers, shareholders and the rest of the community.

The superannuation disaster

Now let's turn to superannuation. In April 1992, the Australian parliament passed the Keating government's *Superannuation Guarantee (Administration) Act*. The legislation compelled employers to pay 3 per cent of their employees' salary into a superannuation fund. Employees wouldn't be able to access that money until they retired.

That legislation ended an argument that had been going on since 1928, when the Bruce government tried to set up a unified national insurance scheme for retirement and sickness and disability. In those days it wasn't called superannuation; it was 'contributory retirement insurance', as opposed to the non-contributory age pension that had been established in 1900 in New South Wales and become national with Federation in 1901. Retirement income plans on top of that pension were provided by employers to a small, privileged and mostly white-collar fraction of the workforce.

Stanley Melbourne Bruce tried to bundle retirement, sickness and disability into one scheme, and in light of what's happened since – Medicare, the superannuation guarantee and finally the National Disability Insurance Scheme – like Peter Smedley, Bruce was well ahead of his time. He established a royal commission in 1923, which took four years to agree with him, and the National Insurance Bill was introduced into parliament in 1928. It was vigorously opposed by employers, who wanted to keep retirement plans as a special benefit for staff, and eventually it lapsed when Bruce was defeated in 1929.

There was another attempt ten years later, when Joe Lyons introduced the National Health and Pensions Bill, which was similar to the Bruce bill of 1928. That actually passed and became law in 1938, but the whole thing was abandoned when the Second World War broke out a year later.

There was no further progress until Gough Whitlam, who came to power in 1972 and a year later established the National

Superannuation Committee of Inquiry under the chairmanship of Keith Hancock, an industrial relations academic. The majority report, which didn't come out until after Whitlam was sacked, recommended merging the age pension into a contributory universal age pension, an idea rejected by Malcolm Fraser in 1979. But the Hancock Inquiry's minority report, written by one Kenneth Hedley, recommended keeping the pension separate and supplementing it with occupational superannuation. This eventually became the basis for Australia's superannuation system.

After that, the unions and the Labor Party really started pushing for superannuation for workers as opposed to just white-collar staff, and it was kicked off by the Storemen and Packers Union with their own fund in the late '70s. It's important to understand that in those days the argument about inequality was entirely focused on industrial relations – in fact, politics itself was essentially a battle between labour and capital, through the Liberal and Labor parties. The unions were tremendously powerful, and led the charge for universal superannuation, as they had been doing since the 1928 bill.

As soon as it was elected in 1983, the Hawke government started trying to do something about wealth and income in retirement. They began by immediately cutting the tax on retirement lump sums to 15 per cent, turning super into a way to avoid tax (a mistake, I think). The process of embedding universal employee super didn't really get going until 1985, when the government asked the Australian Conciliation and Arbitration Commission to include 3 per cent super contributions in industrial awards. This was approved by the commission, but employers challenged it in the High Court. They argued that it wasn't an industrial relations issue and therefore was none of the arbitration commission's business, but they lost the argument.

By 1991, one-third of the workforce still wasn't covered, so Keating, then prime minister, decided to take super one step further.

The federal Budget that year (the unfortunate John Kerin's only one) included the superannuation guarantee legislation, which would move super from awards into law, so everybody would be covered.

The super payment was to be extra money, in place of the pay rise the unions had been demanding – or rather, it was a deferred pay rise, one that could only be spent when the recipient stopped working. So it came from employers, not employees. The government thought an ordinary pay rise would be too inflationary for workers to spend at the time, so in a deal between Keating and ACTU secretary Bill Kelty as part of the Prices and Incomes Accord that had underpinned the government since its election in 1983, it was agreed that employers would pay the amount into 'approved' super funds.

Keating's vision was to extend super to all, but Kelty had other ideas: he wanted to entrench the future of the unions, because he saw membership declining. So each industry sector had its own fund, half owned by the union that covered that industry and half owned by the relevant employer organisation. Dozens of new savings organisations connected to unions came into being over the next few years, with executives, staff, nice offices and boards of trustees taken from the unions and employer bodies. They were all very happy, excitedly creating a new industry and a new future for trade unions.

The whole thing was typical of Paul Keating and the financial reforms he engineered as treasurer in the Hawke government during the 1980s. Those reforms – such as floating the dollar and deregulating banking – had been around for years. They were widely argued about, but governments couldn't bring themselves to implement them. And then Keating and Hawke just got on with it. Many of these things had been recommended in the Campbell Inquiry's 838-page final report, which was presented to Malcolm Fraser in 1981 and then just sat on his desk. The Campbell Inquiry established the intellectual basis for the modernisation of the

Australian economy through financial deregulation, and set us up for decades of economic success. (Campbell did not recommend national super, because he was all about free markets; he wouldn't come at anything so socialist as a national superannuation scheme.)

I was editor of *The Australian Financial Review* throughout most of this time, and it really was a thrilling period to be covering Australian political economy. Every day something new and dramatic was announced, and newspapers were flying off the stands. I used to spend as much time with Paul Keating as I could, listening spellbound as he explained what he was doing and why. I must confess that under my leadership the *AFR* was fully on board with what he and Hawke were doing. I had covered the Campbell Report as the paper's 'Chanticleer' columnist and was excited to see much of it, plus super, finally being implemented.

Keating eventually shoved universal superannuation through with the support of Bill Kelty and the ACTU, not to mention the High Court and the parliament, and declared that we had arrived at the Promised Land. But, with the benefit of hindsight, it was a half-done, supply-side reform based on a cosy, short-term deal, which created compulsory savings – and the institutions and jobs for those who managed them – but left ordinary people exposed to the predations of a rapacious industry. Extending award super to everyone through legislation was definitely a good thing, as was the follow-up legislation in 1993 to set the operating and prudential rules for the super funds, but it didn't go far enough.

Specifically, it didn't sort out what happens to the money in retirement, after it's been saved. Super funds were set up as savings vehicles only, with members left to their own devices in retirement. In other words, what Keating created wasn't really a retirement insurance scheme, but enforced saving. It also had an unnecessary tax break thrown in. After all, if you pass a law compelling something, you don't also need a tax break to encourage it. By cutting the tax on lump sums and super contributions, even though the contributions were compulsory, Keating began the process of turning super into a tax avoidance scheme for rich people and a honey pot for the banks. That process was completed by John Howard and Peter Costello, when they made super lump sums entirely tax-free for people over sixty, and also removed Keating's 'reasonable benefit limits', basically allowing wealthy people to put as much money as they liked into the super tax shelter.

And, like Winnie-the-Pooh, the banks wasted no time hopping into this honeypot, disastrously for all, including themselves. To extend the A.A. Milne analogy a bit further, recall the scene in *Winnie-the-Pooh* when the 'bear of little brain' eats so much honey he gets stuck in Rabbit's front door. This is a bit like what happened to the banks. They ate so much super they became bloated, and got stuck.

Of course, there's nothing inherently wrong with banks dipping their paws into financial honeypots – that's what companies do. The problem is that it wasn't properly regulated. A couple of years ago I challenged Keating about this in an interview onstage at the Sydney Opera House, saying to him: 'Paul, you established a fine system for forcing Australians to save, but then you threw them to the wolves with no regulation controlling those who ended up with the money. Do you accept that now?' The discussion, which had been quite jovial until then, swiftly went downhill – and he didn't answer the question either.

In his defence, Keating might have thought the industry super funds would do a better job of hanging on to members' money when they retired, and providing pensions. Instead, the funds positioned themselves only as savings organisations – and still do. Their job, they believed, was to invest the money until retirement, at which point they handed it over to the member, who then took off with a very fat bank account. It was like winning the lottery.

Most people who win the lottery have no idea what to do with the money, and that's also true of big retirement lump sums. Some people spend it all and then happily go on the government pension, well travelled. But most spend a bit of it and then, intimidated by the largest amount of cash they have ever had their hands on, decide to see a financial adviser they heard about at a barbecue or found on Google.

And until a subsequent Labor government finally passed another law in 2012 banning conflicted remuneration for financial advice, for the first twenty years of Australia's much-vaunted super-annuation system, those advisers to whom the money was handed over at retirement would give it to a wealth manager like AMP or one of the banks – in return for a sales commission. To repeat: they used to get sales commissions, and naturally often gave the money to the company paying the best commission. In other words, the advisers weren't really advisers at all, they were salespeople, selling products. What's more, a lot of the time they were selling the products of the bank or company they worked for. Needless to say, this was not properly revealed: they presented themselves as advisers, or planners, to people who had suddenly come into large sums of money as a result of a legal obligation to save.

I'll get stuck into the advice industry in detail in the next section, but at this point I want to focus on the banks and AMP. Keating's failure to regulate the other side of the superannuation guarantee – that is, how the retirement savings were managed – led to one of the greatest lapses of governance in Australian financial history. The banks and AMP were attracted to superannuation like flies to a cow pat. A lot of people got very rich harvesting big commissions and fees from managing super accounts. And on the flipside, a lot more people have been ripped off – often losing everything, usually losing something and always suffering an opportunity cost. As a consequence, a whole industry – financial services – was corrupted, chasing government-mandated savings without a requirement to put clients' interests first.

In some ways, Keating's laissez-faire vision was simply in tune with the times. While I don't think that excuses the failures, it does put them into some context. 1992 was also the year Francis Fukuyama published his book *The End of History and the Last Man*, expanding on his famous 1989 essay 'The End of History?'. In both the book and the essay, Fukuyama argued: 'What we may be witnessing is not just the end of the Cold War, or the passing of a particular period of post-war history, but the end of history as such: that is, the end point of mankind's ideological evolution and the universalization of Western liberal democracy as the final form of human government.'

In some ways that article was just an example of the power of headlines. The title 'The End of History?' struck a chord, especially since it was followed just a few months later by the collapse of the Berlin Wall. It captured the historic power of that moment. It's hard to remember, or believe, now, with the GFC and the rise of (still) communist China behind us, but it all seemed pretty conclusive back then, that liberal democracy and free-market capitalism had triumphed, and that government control was definitely on the way out. Fukuyama's essay was published in 1989, but it wasn't until 1 February 1992 that Boris Yeltsin and George H.W. Bush met at Camp David and formally declared that the Cold War had ended.

In his 2018 book *21 Lessons for the 21st Century*, Yuval Noah Harari describes what happened like this:

> during the 20th century the global elites in New York, London, Berlin and Moscow formulated three grand stories that claimed to explain the whole past and to predict the future of the entire world: the fascist story, the communist story and the liberal story. The Second World War knocked

out the fascist story, and from the 1940s to the late 1980s, the world became a battleground between just two stories: communism and liberalism.

The communist story collapsed and the liberal story remained the dominant guide to the human past and the indispensable manual for the future of the world – or so it seemed to the global elite.

In 1992, 'economic rationalism', as it was called by its critics in the union movement and elsewhere, was rampant. Ronald Reagan had finished two terms as US president and Margaret Thatcher had completed eleven years as prime minister of the United Kingdom. Both of them were advised by Milton Friedman, the immensely influential American economist who won the 1976 Nobel Prize. Friedman became the intellectual guru of the wave of free-market thinking that accompanied Reagan and Thatcher. He took the great Scottish economist Adam Smith's idea of the 'invisible hand' of the market and stretched it to breaking point. Some of his more famous lines are:

The society that puts equality before freedom will end up with neither.

Underlying most arguments against the free market is a lack of belief in freedom itself.

I am in favor of cutting taxes under any circumstances and for any excuse, for any reason, whenever it's possible.

The government solution to a problem is usually as bad as the problem.

Friedman's ideas fitted perfectly with the collapse of the Soviet Union and the mood of the times, and Reagan and Thatcher adopted them enthusiastically. Laissez-faire capitalism and faith in the market were ascendant everywhere, and the impact on Australian economic policy was enormous. Even Australia's supposedly (according to its own constitution) socialist Labor government, under former union boss Bob Hawke, became one of the world's leading exponents of market-based deregulation and other neo-liberal ideas. Enterprise bargaining replaced centralised wage fixing; the Australian dollar was floated; bank ownership was largely unfettered. It was a thrilling time for economic reformists (and journalists), but some things were missed because it was assumed that the market was more or less perfect and could be trusted to iron things out.

What does all this have to do with Australia's banks and the superannuation guarantee legislation? Plenty. Government-mandated savings, as legislated by the Keating government, went against the mood of the times – hadn't the headquarters of central planning and socialism just collapsed? And wasn't it clear that the free market was now the only way to go? Government businesses were being sold like ice-creams on a hot day and deregulation was the byword of governments everywhere, so there was a definite limit to how far the Labor government could push what seemed like a socialist agenda on superannuation.

In this environment, creating a mandatory savings regime and giving trade unions a major piece of it only made sense in the context of the industrial relations deal-making that went on within the Prices and Incomes Accord, and the close relationship between the ALP and the union movement. But regulating – or even nationalising – the industry that invests the money? Of course not. Don't be silly. The 'socialism' of mandated savings had to be balanced by a fully deregulated industry to manage the money.

The result was the creation of a huge, largely unregulated industry that fed off government-mandated savings and quickly became very rich indeed. Naturally the banks wanted in. Which brings me to the next significant event of 1992 in the development of Australia's flawed financial services industry.

A world-class salary

The last of the three significant things that happened in 1992 was Westpac's recruitment as CEO of Robert L. Joss, vice-chairman of Wells Fargo Bank in San Francisco.

At fifty-one, Bob Joss had had a 21-year career at Wells Fargo, with additional stints in the White House and the US Treasury. But it looked like he was going to miss out on the American bank's top job because he was the same age as the first man in line, so word reached Westpac chairman John Uhrig that Joss might be a good choice to steer Westpac out of a near-death experience.

In 1992, Westpac had reported a loss of $1.56 billion and wiped out almost half its shareholders' funds, with $2.7 billion in bad debts write-offs. The recession and commercial property collapse of 1990 had hurt many financial institutions and sent a few to the wall. Of the big four banks, Westpac was hardest hit. It was the closest any of them have ever come to going broke, including during the GFC sixteen years later. Kerry Packer took advantage of the collapse in Westpac's share price to buy 10 per cent of the bank, and got himself appointed to its board.

At the end of 1992, the Westpac board was desperate for a saviour. Under pressure from Packer, they had forced out the previous CEO, Frank Conroy, and felt they needed to appoint a world-class banker to lead them out of the wilderness. They decided to go for Bob Joss.

A contact at management consulting firm McKinsey & Co., whom they knew was a friend of Joss's, made the approach on

Christmas Eve 1992, suggesting that he consider Westpac's advances seriously. At first he wasn't inclined to do any such thing. 'I thought this was madness,' Joss said later. 'Why would I want to get involved in that?' Two weeks later, in early January, John Uhrig flew to Los Angeles to meet Joss at LA airport and formally offered him the job. A few days after that, Joss flew to Australia, checking into a hotel under a false name to avoid suspicion, and met with the rest of the Westpac board, as well as the governor of the Reserve Bank, Bernie Fraser. And then he accepted the job, with no more due diligence than that, starting work on 10 February 1993.

Joss was a fine banker and a widely admired bloke – a good appointment, as it turned out, and he really did turn Westpac around. He even received an Order of Australia in 2016. From the date he was appointed to the market peak in 2007, Westpac was the best-performing of the big four banks, although admittedly it was coming from well behind.

The only problem is that Joss was paid more than the CEOs of the other three major banks, combined. In 1995 – the earliest year for which we still have records – Joss's salary was close to $2 million, double the salary of the next highest-paid executive at Westpac. I was editor of *The Age* at the time, so not as closely involved in business reporting as I had been before, but I well remember Joss's wage being a big deal – a shockwave through the banking industry, and corporate Australia generally, that reverberated for a long time. Within three years of his appointment, all the other big bank CEOs were on more than a million: in 1995–96, David Murray at the Commonwealth Bank, Don Argus at NAB and Don Mercer at ANZ each got pay rises of around $500,000, taking them to $1.3 million, on their way to matching Bob Joss within a year or two.

You don't need a vivid imagination to conjure up the boardroom discussions that would have taken place in those other banks:

how it's a competitive marketplace for talent and they wouldn't be able to attract the best people if they didn't pay world-class salaries, that the prestige of the bank and its board would be diminished if it was seen to be a poor payer … and possibly even a few undignified tantrums – 'It's not fair!' Whatever the internal reasoning and arguments, the other banks soon caught up with what Westpac was paying Bob Joss, and their big corporate customers started catching up as well. It's not going too far to say that Joss's appointment was a bonanza for corporate bosses in Australia. US executive pay had arrived in Australia.

It would have happened anyway, of course; if it wasn't Westpac and Joss, another company would have got into enough trouble that they felt the need to pay whatever it took to get a top American. The huge salaries being paid in the United States were always going to flow to the rest of the world eventually, at least to some extent. But the point is that it was one of the banks that kicked this trend off in Australia, and I believe that from that moment on running a bank became not simply a way to cap off a career, get a knighthood/AO and invitations to the best dinner parties, but a way to get rich. There is a big difference between retiring with $5 million and retiring with $50 million; building an eight-figure sum of capital is very hard to do, and has traditionally been the preserve of entrepreneurs who created businesses and sold them, or property developers like Frank Lowy and John Gandel – in other words, people who take risks. It wasn't the world of more or less risk-free company executives: they used to retire on a comfortable pension and the satisfaction of a job well done – until Bob Joss came to town.

There was soon another event that further super-charged executive salaries. Until this point, executive salaries were coyly published in 'bands', with no names attached. Annual reports simply revealed how many executives were sitting in each $10,000 band.

To find out what we thought was the CEO's salary, we just went to the top band in each report, where the figure '1' sat all alone beside the largest number.

After 1998, the full salaries – including cash and bonuses – of all senior executives and directors had to be disclosed, with names attached to numbers. It seemed like a good idea at the time, but it turned out to be another bonanza for executives, because no self-respecting board of directors wanted to be in the bottom quartile of payers. It was a matter of pride, as well as competition for talent. Every bank – every company – wanted to be in the top quartile, so it became a bit like Garrison Keillor's Lake Wobegon, where all the children are above average. With everyone trying to crowd into the top quartile, salaries were rapidly pushed higher and higher. It arrived at peak greed in 2010, when the Commonwealth Bank's Ralph Norris scored $16.1 million, more than 800 times average weekly earnings.

Why am I going on about salaries so much? Because when people started climbing the corporate ladder not for the love of it – that is, love of the business, the job, the chase, the prestige – but because it was a great way to get rich, something profoundly negative happened to the cultures of big companies. And banks were in the vanguard of this shift.

At this point we need to bring Mr Friedman back into the discussion, along with the prevailing economics – the zeitgeist – of the times. One of Milton Friedman's main propositions, along with his ideas that 'inflation is always and everywhere a monetary phenomenon' and governments are always hopeless at virtually everything, was that the only purpose of companies was to make a profit. In time, that became the obligation to maximise shareholders' value. In Friedman's book *Capitalism and Freedom*, originally published in 1962 but hugely influential in the late 1980s, he argued: 'There is one and only one social responsibility of business – to use its resources and engage in activities designed to increase its profits so long as it stays within the rules of the game, which is to say, engages in open and free competition without deception or fraud.' In other words, he argued that companies have no responsibility to society, beyond their responsibility to make money. He went even further, arguing that when companies concern themselves with the community rather than focusing on profits, it entails a loss of individual freedom, a loss that in the end leads to totalitarianism. Friedman's philosophy affected how companies saw their own mission. Instead of their purpose being to make cars, for instance, or mine iron ore, companies started defining their purpose solely as making money and enhancing their shareholders' wealth. It seemed to be the thing to do, and naturally shareholders were all in favour of that – especially the financial institutions, which were becoming very powerful then.

This pure, free-market approach to corporations was enthusiastically adopted by those running them, especially financial firms, whose actual purpose involved money. In a way, Friedman had created an environment that allowed the finance sector to invade industry – for Wall Street to take over Main Street, as they say in the United States. An early example of that (from 1988) was Kohlberg Kravis Roberts' leveraged buyout of RJR Nabisco, memorably described in the 1989 book *Barbarians at the Gate* and the 1993 TV movie of the same name. The same ideas were captured – and satirised – in the 1987 movie *Wall Street*, starring Michael Douglas as investment banker Gordon Gekko.

Like Donald Horne's *The Lucky Country*, *Wall Street* was meant as satire but widely taken as truth. In the movie, Michael Douglas's character addresses shareholders at the annual meeting of Teldar Paper, a fictional, venerable old US paper company. He observes that the company has thirty-three vice-presidents, each earning more than US$200,000 per year. 'Now, I have spent the last two months analysing what all these guys do, and I still can't figure it out,' he says. 'The new law of evolution in corporate America seems to be survival of the unfittest.' He goes on to declare that 'I am not a destroyer of companies. I am a liberator of them', and then the clincher: 'The point is, ladies and gentlemen, that greed, for lack of a better word, is good. Greed is right, greed works. Greed clarifies, cuts through, and captures the essence of the evolutionary spirit.'

This idea that greed is good captured the essence of both Darwinism and Adam Smith's 'invisible hand', and it fitted perfectly with the mood of the time, since capitalism and freedom were seen to have triumphed over socialism and repression. Even China was adopting market-based reforms, and the 'visible hand' of the Soviet Union's price controls was formally abolished on 2 January 1992. The satire in the phrase 'greed is good' got lost.

So there was plenty of intellectual and social support for the idea that corporations – the engines of capitalism and liberalism – needed to focus on making money, and other considerations could take a back seat. Since greed was good, it followed that the best way to make sure company executives were sufficiently focused on profit was through money as well. Step one, make them greedy. Step two, give them a pathway to riches that depends on maximising shareholder wealth – that is, increasing company profits and therefore share prices.

The problem is that in the real world shareholders don't bear all the risks in a business. Employees, suppliers and the communities in which the companies operate also bear a lot of risk. What's more, stock markets allow shareholders to diversify their risks across different classes of assets and across companies around the world, something employees and other local stakeholders can't hope to do. So by focusing the purpose of the corporation on shareholders alone, the directors and executives are in fact serving those who are least committed to them. Unlike employees and local communities and, in many cases, customers, shareholders can, and do, sell out at any time.

Nevertheless, from the late 1980s and '90s onwards, not only did executive salaries soar, but elaborate bonus schemes were constructed, with short-term incentives (STIs) and long-term incentives (LTIs), aimed at 'paying for performance' (defined as higher profits and share prices). What was actually just a simple carrot was wrapped in the special pseudo-science that keeps expensive remuneration consultants in clover. The remuneration sections of annual reports ballooned, and many companies lost what we now call their moral compass. I'm not suggesting for a moment that before the 1990s all companies were highly moral and never behaved unethically, but a shift did occur then – for the worse. And banks were, and are, especially vulnerable to this moral decay for two main reasons.

First, because they had absorbed the succubae of wealth management businesses, with sales cultures that conflicted with, and then fundamentally changed, their own more austere credit-rationing cultures. And second, because of the crucial distinction between financial services businesses and all others: we give them our money to look after. Usually when we buy a product or service, we pay for it by physically handing money over, either at the time or in response to an invoice a bit later (payment in seven days, please!). But with banks and fund managers and financial advisers, we give them all our money, which makes them uniquely unaccountable. Instead of sending us a bill, they can and do just extract money, whether in the form of fixed or percentage fees, directly from our account.

By handing over your money to bankers and advisers, you expose yourself to multiple risks. The most obvious one is that an unscrupulous custodian – or one who is just going through a tough period, perhaps because of gambling or divorce – might simply steal your money. Because the temptation can be as great as the opportunity, bankers and financial advisers need to be especially ethical and upright people. Most of them are indeed ethical and upright, but unfortunately many are not. And as with burglars and drunk drivers, laws and regulations are designed not for honest, sober people, but for the crooks and drunks. In financial services, our laws and regulations have failed to protect us from misbehaviour – and nor have they protected us from deeper problems in the financial system, as Australian banking's 'perfect storm' demonstrates.

The perfect storm

The movie *The Perfect Storm* came out the same year the Commonwealth Bank took over Colonial – 2000. In the film, the crew of a fishing boat, the *Andrea Gail*, handsomely captained by George Clooney, decide to go out into a gathering storm. Unfortunately, it turns out to be a rare confluence of three storms, not one, and the boat and all those on board are lost, after riding up and then being swamped by a memorably large wave.

The perfect storm for Australian banks was also the confluence of three winds: the unregulated superannuation system set up by Paul Keating and ACTU chief Bill Kelty; the idea that financial supermarkets – banking, super and life insurance – were a good idea; and the explosion in executive salaries combined with the sole focus of companies on making money for shareholders and executives.

There was one final event that sealed the banks' fate, culturally at least: it was the financial system inquiry headed by David Murray, which delivered its report to the government in 2014. Murray had by then become a sort of supreme godfather of the financial services sector – today we would call him a 'thought leader' – having been CEO of the Commonwealth Bank and having established the Australian Government Future Fund, an independently managed fund into which the government deposits funds for the future payment of superannuation to retired civil servants. His central recommendation and key theme was that the banks needed to be 'unquestionably strong'. He basically told the regulator, APRA (the Australian Prudential Regulation Authority), to raise the banks' capital ratios (meaning the amount of money they hold in reserve) to achieve that end. It was a misdirection. Not only were the banks already unquestionably strong, but Murray ensured that bank regulation remained focused on profits and capital strength rather than customer outcomes and competition. In other words, in the face of growing evidence that the banks' biggest problem was the way they were treating customers, Murray said, 'No, no, the biggest problem is their strength and stability – focus on that, not the customers.' 'Consumer outcomes', as he called them, came well down the report, and the recommendations were vague – for example: 'Introduce a targeted and principles-based product design and distribution obligation.' APRA and the banks were only too happy with that.

By that stage it was probably too late to change the direction of bank behaviour and regulation before the ordure hit the fan – it was already in the air, heading for the rotating blades. By 2014, more and more stories were coming out about appalling consumer outcomes, and calls for a royal commission were becoming insistent, but the Murray Inquiry ignored all that, instead puffing fresh wind into the sails of the banking industry's *Andrea Gail* as it sailed into its perfect storm. The wave came in the form of the Hayne Royal Commission, which I will examine in Chapter 3. But first let's shine a spotlight on financial advisers.

2

The Advisers

THIS IS WHERE THE STORY GETS MORE PERSONAL. I was fired as editor of *The Age* in 1995 because circulation was falling and I couldn't turn it around – the team was losing, so naturally it was time to sack the coach. In fact, it turned out to be the start of the long decline in newspaper sales caused by the internet, which is still continuing. Anyway, I returned, slightly bruised, to being a reporter and columnist for the ABC and Fairfax, chalking it up as part of life's rich tapestry.

As a finance journalist, I'd started out reporting on the 'big end of town': the stock exchange, big mergers and acquisitions, and the strategies of Australia's corporate giants. In the late '90s I was caught up reporting the great waterfront dispute in Melbourne as well as the big corporate and stock market stories of the time, but in the early 2000s, when I moved from the *Financial Review* to *The Age* and *The Sydney Morning Herald*, I shifted focus to personal finance and started looking for the first time at superannuation, personal investment, financial advice and the many challenges, both local and global, faced by those trying to prepare for their retirement.

I was amazed, and more than a bit horrified, to discover that the whole thing was based on deliberate conflicts of interest: those whom we thought were advisers were actually salespeople on commission. The shoddy treatment of shareholders by directors at the big end of town was a field of daisies compared to what was happening to ordinary people trying to find a way to have their life savings looked after. They were being harvested by financial advisers and the wealth management industry as a matter of routine, like so many ripe ears of corn. It was terrible and – for a journalist with a fairly well-honed sense of right and wrong – irresistible as a story.

Saving wisely for the future, putting your trust in a financial adviser, implementing a financial plan: these are the mainstays of personal finance, and they are life-shaping decisions, some of the most important any of us will ever make. Yet the industry that was created to support us in those decisions, I discovered, was actually designed to sell us things – to distribute products, not to provide independent advice – while carefully concealing that fact, calling the salespeople 'advisers'. How did this happen, and how should people approach those important financial decisions while navigating an industry that's mostly trying to clean them out? Answering that question became my focus.

I started to become a little bit obsessed with the disconnect between what the industry knew it was doing and what consumers thought was going on. The real job of a financial planner – as they and their employers understood it – was to distribute investment products. They called their organisations 'dealer groups', and still do. AMP and the banks called the financial planning networks 'advice-based distribution'. Planners were, and to some extent still are, paid for performance – not investment performance but the volume of sales.

That was not what most, if not all, consumers understood to be happening. They thought they were getting financial advice. Doesn't the sign on the door say 'Financial Adviser'? And isn't there a certificate on the wall saying this person's qualified? Yes, and yes. And the planner always spins an excellent web of fancy talk about 'risk tolerance' and what's happening with the markets, and some of the important principles of investing. But it's really like talking to a TV salesperson at JB Hi-Fi or a car salesperson at the local Toyota dealer: they know what they're talking about, and sometimes they're brilliant at it, but their job is to sell you something.

The business of financial advice and investment is important, second only to our health, but it is also complex and difficult to navigate, and it wasn't set up for our benefit. As we've learnt from the Hayne Royal Commission, not only is the financial advice industry full of traps and pitfalls, it's crowded with advisers, planners, brokers, bankers and salespeople who are looking after their own interests, vying for a slice of our money. Not all are like that, or even most of them, but it's hard to know the difference between the trustworthy and the unscrupulous – and in any case the system has been stacked against us.

So I started writing columns about all this, and specifically about the problem of financial advisers getting commissions from banks and wealth managers while presenting themselves as independent. I even entered the lions' dens a few times and told them directly, in poorly received speeches. My message was: you will never be seen as a truly professional industry unless you ditch sales commissions. I believed that financial advisers themselves were also big losers from their sector's sales culture, and that if they wanted to be respected in the long term they needed to switch their professional focus to clients, not those whose products they were distributing. Most didn't want to hear that. Instead, they focused on my accusation of conflicts of interest and corrupt practices. 'You're tarring us all with the same brush,' came the cry from the industry. 'Most of us do look after our clients' interests!'

And that's probably true – most financial planners are, and have always been, fundamentally honest people trying to do the best for their clients. Not all of them are spivvy salespeople with tans and gold chains chasing commissions (back then) and fees now. But as I saw it there were two issues: it wasn't about the individuals – the system was broken; and even the most ethical financial planner will usually put his or her own family first when it comes to the crunch. Most people do. And advisers are all – to a man and woman – thinking about their own retirement, as they help clients with theirs. For most of them, their advice practice is their super and its value is determined by the size of the 'fee book' or the 'funds under advice'. Selling the practice back to the licence holder (AMP or a bank) under the normal 'buyer of last resort' arrangement that they all have in place is their retirement lump sum: the way to have a comfortable retirement is to have the greatest number of clients paying the highest possible fees and commissions.

But how did such an obviously flawed system develop?

In the early days especially, most of the financial advisers used to be life insurance salespeople. Before the 1980s, there were three sorts of financial advisers: bank managers, accountants and life insurance agents, and in some ways the last of them had the best relationship with ordinary people. Unlike the other two, who sat austere in their offices, life agents went to people's homes and got to know them. I remember when I was young our family became quite friendly with one insurance salesman, and so did I when I was buying my own life insurance after getting married and having children. They were often members of the Masons, Rotary or Lion's Club; in most communities the AMP agent was a pillar of society. Why did life insurance agents work so hard to make a sale? Because most people didn't automatically get a life policy, as they got a car or a TV; life insurance had to be actively sold, and the agents were paid sales commissions, usually equal to the first year's premium. Bank managers and accountants, on the other hand, were paid by the hour, whether they 'sold' something or not.

As the market for superannuation and post-retirement investment products grew rapidly after the super guarantee legislation of 1992, and AMP and the banks started moving into those businesses, someone had to sell the products. Who better than the life insurance agents? And naturally enough, the commission-based sales culture of life insurance transferred to investment products. It didn't have to be that way, but the products had to be sold and the life insurance agents were used to getting commissions, so it was a natural thing to just keep that system going.

As a result, the first set of regulations around financial advice were based on the idea that it was all about the products, not the advice or the advisers who were selling them. Advisers were required to know their products, but not necessarily to know their clients.

At the same time, the series of privatisations and demutualisations (Commonwealth Bank, Telstra, CSL, Qantas, AMP and NRMA Insurance) introduced many ordinary Australians to the business of share ownership, and therefore the need for financial advice.

There were four opportunities to fix the original regulatory mistakes and change what was always going to end up as a flawed, corrupt system for providing financial advice, but on each occasion the people involved failed to do it. The four big regulatory failures were:

1. the Labor government's decision in 1992 to legislate mandatory retirement savings without properly regulating the industry that holds the money
2. the complete failure of the financial system inquiry chaired by former Amcor managing director Stan Wallis in the mid-1990s to recognise the need for proper regulation
3. the decision by Treasury in 1997 to regulate superannuation and insurance as if they were securities, and to licence firms rather than individuals
4. the failure of yet another financial system inquiry, the one chaired by the former CEO of the Commonwealth Bank David Murray, in 2013–14, to bring financial services under consumer protection regulations.

All of the inquiries and reports and regulatory decisions through the years were made by players in the game who had little to lose and everything to gain by doing nothing and protecting the status quo – union officials looking to expand their power; bureaucrats with defined benefit super schemes who therefore already knew they'd be fine in retirement; and above all industrialists, bankers and lawyers who wanted the system to remain largely unregulated. They were philosophically and personally committed to free markets, and none actually had a direct stake in the outcome of their decisions. In fact, none of the people on the various panels – not one! – was there specifically to represent consumers.

In the late 1990s, apart from the waterfront dispute, I was also reporting on the 1996–97 financial system inquiry chaired by Wallis. It was meant to be an update of the earlier inquiry into the financial system headed by Keith Campbell, appointed in 1979 by the treasurer at the time, John Howard.

A quick note on the Campbell Committee. Keith Campbell was chairman and CEO of the property developer Hooker

Corporation, and the other panellists included the chief of AMP, Alan Coates, plus a financial adviser named Keith Halkerston and a couple of bureaucrats. Their work was hugely influential, providing the intellectual foundations of the Hawke government's financial sector reforms in the 1980s – after being supported by yet another review, the Martin Inquiry, in 1983. Campbell established a deregulatory starting point for thinking about government involvement in the financial system. In its final report, the committee describes its approach to reform thus: 'to take the present system as its starting point and to assess the usefulness of each existing case of government intervention by asking whether it would be advantageous to remove it from the system'. Not that the Campbell Committee was in favour of a fully deregulated system. In 1979–80 the full impact of Reaganism and Thatcherism had not quite been felt on these shores, so the Campbell Report also said: 'The Committee recognises that a policy change cannot be supported simply because it represents a move towards freer competition. Attention is drawn to the dangers of carrying out reform in an ad hoc piecemeal fashion.' But the main thrust of the report was to minimise regulation, as you might expect from a property developer.

Sixteen years and a financial revolution later, newly elected prime minister John Howard decided that another look at the financial system was required, to update Campbell, which had been more or less fully implemented by the Labor government he replaced. So he turned to Australia's leading manufacturer, Stan Wallis; a lawyer and merchant banker named Bill Beerworth; Linda Nicholls, a company director and former banker; Jeff Carmichael, who was an academic and former Reserve Bank official; and Ian Harper, also an academic and former director of the Reserve Bank. They were asked to 'report on the results of financial deregulation flowing from the Campbell Report published in 1981', but it's pretty clear from the title they chose for the overview of their their 1997 final report – *The Financial System: Towards 2010* – that they wanted to be seen as looking ahead to the future rather than reviewing the past. (I think they had in mind Arthur C. Clarke's 1982 novel *2010: Odyssey Two*, which was his sequel to *2001: A Space Odyssey*, but I'm afraid the allusion was lost on many.) The report talks about the debate between those who think that change in the financial system is likely to be gradual and incremental and those who think, then, that a paradigm shift is underway – 'a sharp discontinuity from the trend experience of the past'.

And then it concludes: 'The Inquiry is unable to resolve this debate. However, it considers that it does not need to base its recommendations on firm or precise predictions about the future of the financial system. Creating the future and securing a place in it is a role for the private sector responding to customer demands. Provided processes are genuinely competitive, the private sector is best placed to determine the future shape of the financial system.'

In short, and totally unsurprisingly given the personnel involved, Wallis came down in favour of less regulation, not more: 'Like the Campbell Committee before it, the Inquiry has proceeded in the knowledge that the performance of the financial system relies heavily on maintaining free and competitive markets.' Among other things, Wallis recommended that Australia's fragmented regulation of the financial sector be brought under one roof, and that the Australian Securities Commission and parts of the Insurance and Superannuation Commission be combined into something called the Corporations and Financial Services Commission (CFSC). The government, flexing a tiny bit of independence, ended up calling it the Australian Securities and Investments Commission (ASIC), but it was the same thing.

The committee also recommended that bank supervision be taken away from the Reserve Bank and given to a new regulator called the Australian Prudential Regulatory Commission. Again the government went a bit rogue and called it a Regulation Authority – APRA – but it was same thing.

More broadly, Wallis reflected the prevailing view at the time, that deregulation and competition would deal with all inefficiencies and mispricing – that the market would sort things out and bring prices down and that consumers would win. It was a naive view. What Wallis didn't count on was the banks swooping in and taking control of the whole set-up. As the Reserve Bank later commented (in its 2014 submission to the Murray Inquiry), Wallis underestimated the banks' capacity to expand and 'acquire businesses along their supply chain'. And as the Hayne royal commission said in its interim report, while customers might enjoy the convenience of a 'one-stop shop' for financial services, it 'does not necessarily produce efficiency in outcomes for customers. The one-stop shop has an incentive to promote the owner's products above others, even where they may not be ideal for the consumer.'

Crucially, Wallis recommended that financial consumer protection be moved from the Australian Competition and Consumer Commission (ACCC) to ASIC (which it was calling the CFSC), setting up two classes of consumer protection regulations. (As we would learn during the royal commission in 2018, unlike the ACCC, ASIC got too close to the companies it was meant to be supervising and ended up in cosy deals with them, rather than coming down hard on them to protect consumers.)

The other thing I remember reporting on in the late 1990s, without understanding its future significance, was a beast called CLERP 6, which stood for Corporate Law Economic Reform Program No. 6. This was a reform scheme run entirely by the federal Treasury. Like most other finance journalists at the time, my eyes used to glaze over every time I had a look at the subject. But looking back on it, I now understand that it was actually very important and that the boffins at Treasury, using the Wallis Report as a manual for reform, made two very large and far-reaching mistakes.

First, it was decided that the law covering the distribution of insurance and superannuation would be brought into the regulation of securities, which was needed to go with the creation of ASIC, and second, Treasury decided that the intermediaries – that is, the advisers – would be regulated and licensed at the level of the firm rather than the individual. This was largely based on the ideas contained in the Wallis Report, as was the moving of consumer protection from the ACCC to ASIC.

The significance of these decisions cannot be overstated, and the most significant element of it was that ASIC's regulation of securities, mainly company shares, was based on disclosure – that is, as long as companies fully disclosed their audited financial reports and any other material events, it was 'let the buyer beware'. So naturally, when ASIC and Treasury turned their attention to the regulation of insurance, investment and superannuation products, it was also based on disclosure, through voluminous product disclosure statements (PDSs) and financial services guides (FSGs). Only problem: nobody read them.

What they all failed to realise (or perhaps they just decided to ignore the obvious) was that the people at whom those documents were aimed had no idea how to read them and no inclination to do so. I realised at the time – and wrote in several columns – that the disclosure documentation for financial and investment products was designed *not* to be read. That is, the companies pushing the financial products made sure their PDSs and FSGs were long, boring and dense, so no one would be bothered wading through them. 'Here's our PDS and FSG,' the trusted adviser would say, 'but don't worry about reading it, it's all pretty standard.' And of course, most people trusted their advisers and didn't bother reading such daunting fine print. And even if they had, they wouldn't really have understood them.

Apart from the absurdity of a financial regulatory regime based on disclosure, insurance and superannuation products are not like securities at all, and it's a mistake to treat them the same way. Insurance and super products are bought with a specific event in mind – damage, injury or death in the case of insurance, and retirement in the case of superannuation – and they are sold by sales agents rather than independent brokers as company shares are (although brokers aren't all that independent most of the time either, let's face it).

But perhaps the greatest stuff-up of all in the development of financial advice was the licensing of firms rather than individuals and the failure to decree that advisers had to be independent from the companies issuing the products. The licensing regime was set up that way so that ASIC could more efficiently regulate the industry, dealing with a few large firms rather than individuals, and independence wasn't enforced because Treasury was over-confident in the operation of the market with what it believed was full disclosure. In fact, the disclosure was a sham because it was never read, and the market simply didn't work.

Wallis's twelfth recommendation was: 'Licences should be issued to financial institutions (where the provider of sales and advice acts on behalf of an institution) or to independent advisers (firms or individuals acting on behalf of a client). These would replace existing arrangements for investment advisers, life agents and life brokers. Financial institutions and fund managers wishing to sell retail financial products, including DTIs and life companies, would also need to obtain this licence.' That was the end of individual licences; nobody went for them anymore. From the late '90s onwards, all financial advice licences were issued to firms and institutions; individual advisers were either employees or sub-agents. And note, by the way, that it was explicitly acceptable for financial institutions, including banks (DTIs stands for deposit-taking institutions) to hold advice licences and to employ 'advisers'.

What an absolute shocker! Can you imagine a medical regulation system in which companies employing doctors were licensed rather than the doctors themselves, and in which it was acceptable for the companies holding the licences to be owned by drug companies, so that doctors in effect worked for them? Then add in sales commissions paid by drug companies to doctors for 'selling' their products and you start to understand the system that the geniuses in the Australian government had come up with, legitimised by the Wallis Committee.

The financial system and the health system are comparable: physical health and financial health are enormously important to our wellbeing, but complex for us to handle ourselves. Finance and medicine are equally daunting for most people. But in the medical system, doctors have to study for years and they are individually licensed: if anyone breaches the rules by, say, getting a kickback from a drug company, they're out. Nobody who was designing financial regulation in the 1990s seems to have thought of that. Most people know as much about their health as they do about their finances, but they can rely on trusted, well-qualified and individually regulated doctors to deal with their medical issues. In contrast, not only are financial 'doctors' allowed to be employed by the equivalent of drug companies, but the cost of consulting them often runs into the thousands of dollars and is unsubsidised. A visit to a doctor can cost less than $100, and you get most of it back from Medicare.

Before commissions were banned, financial planners were getting as much as a 10 per cent upfront commission from the promoters of investment products, which is $100,000 on a million-dollar investment. There were also trailing commissions: 1 to 2 per cent per annum, ongoing, or $10,000 to 20,000 a year, forever.

Even now, those sorts of fees are still being extracted from clients' accounts on a 'fee for service' basis rather than sales commissions. For most retirees, it is the most expensive service they buy, by a long way, yet what they get is a fairly passive investment service by someone who might have a diploma and who meets them once a year, if they're lucky.

This was a colossal failure of regulation by a bunch of men and women who were pretty comfortable with their own financial affairs and who failed to put themselves in the shoes of ordinary people who didn't have their level of wealth or understanding about how the financial system worked. They were all well-off individuals, who were relaxed in making big financial decisions as long as all the information was available to them, so that's the system they set up for everybody else. It was a disaster. They simply didn't understand that for most people their finances are as incomprehensible as their health, and they need support from practitioners who are, like doctors, individually licensed and independent from the products they prescribe.

And then finally, there's the financial system inquiry of 2014, headed by David Murray. Looked at in its entirety, the Murray Report is a throwback to the early '90s, a sort of last hurrah of the Milton Friedman free marketeers. In reality, none of the succession of financial system inquiries over the past forty years has done anything other than push deregulation and competition. Hancock, Campbell, Martin, Wallis and Murray were all 'of the business, by the business, for the business'. Customers who could be bothered flung angry, heartfelt one-page submissions at all of them, but the big, well-researched submissions, the ones that were taken notice of, came from the banks and their lobbyists.

Murray was appointed by Treasurer Joe Hockey three months and thirteen days after the 2013 election, won by the Coalition led by Tony Abbott. Murray's final report was delivered to

Hockey in the dying days of Abbott's leadership (and Hockey's treasurership, as it turned out). A month later, Abbott knighted Prince Philip, Duke of Edinburgh, sealing his fate – and by the time the government actually responded to the report, the treasurer was Scott Morrison, in training to be prime minister himself.

All the big financial system inquiries that ended up being such damaging failures – Campbell, Wallis and Murray – were appointed by Coalition governments. I don't believe this is a coincidence. The conservative parties were looking for intellectual support for what they wanted to do anyway, and they always followed the dictum: never start an inquiry unless you know ahead of time what the answer will be. The big exception to this, of course, is the royal commission of 2017–18.

The key word in the Murray Report and in Morrison's response was 'resilience' – the banks had to be 'unquestionably strong'. In essence, Murray – the former lifelong banker – wanted the banks to have more capital, and that's more or less it. Yes, consumers got a mention, but they were secondary, and most importantly Murray gave no more than a passing glance at what is clearly the most important part of the financial system for consumers, and the most in need of reform: the financial advice industry. By comparison, in my view, the amount of capital the banks had was barely relevant.

Tellingly, the section on 'consumer outcomes' refers repeatedly to 'product distribution', and the key recommendation, Number 21, says: 'Introduce a targeted and principles-based product design and distribution obligation.' It goes on to explain: 'The obligation would require product issuers and distributors to consider a range of factors when designing products and distribution strategies. In addition to commercial considerations, issuers and distributors should consider the type of consumer whose financial needs would be addressed by buying the product and the channel best suited to distributing the product.' In other words, in 2014 Murray was still referring to financial advisers as 'product distributors'. He totally missed the opportunity to recommend a properly independent financial advice industry modelled on the health sector, where doctors prescribe drugs but are not 'product distributors'. Now he is – aptly – chairman of AMP, whose business model is entirely based on using financial advisers as product distributors, and is therefore in big trouble because those days are gone. After the royal commission, advisers can no longer be salespeople.

Two years later, and twenty years after Wallis, the financial services industry is foundering in a swamp partly of its own making, but mostly one that was designed and built by bureaucrats and industrialists who either didn't understand what they were doing or didn't care. As a result, banking and investment services are exposed in a structure that is unfit for purpose and that caused the scandals that led to the royal commission. Yes, individual bank executives and advisers did the misdeeds, but it was the regulatory structure set up in the 1990s and confirmed in multiple reviews and inquiries that enabled them. The scandals were inevitable, and they point to the importance of proper regulatory design.

Between 2008 and 2013 there were no less than thirty-five separate inquiries and reports into financial advice and superannuation – parliamentary committees, ASIC reviews and consultations, Treasury consultations and exposure drafts, and committees of inquiry – and, with the benefit of hindsight informed by the royal commission, most of them missed the point. So it's not as if there weren't any opportunities for politicians, bureaucrats and banks to make out the writing on the wall.

In 2003, ASIC produced a damning report on the quality of financial advice, and a few years after that the Financial Planning Association actually banned commissions for its own members, although they represented less than half of the industry. (By the way, according to ASIC, 85 per cent of advisers in those days were either employed by or associated with a product promoter.) In 2009, the Labor government announced that it would ban sales commissions for all financial advisers, and in the same year investigative journalist Adele Ferguson turned her attention to the financial planning industry. She wrote a series of shocking articles about what was going on, which culminated in a Senate inquiry in 2013 that, in 2014, recommended a royal commission into the industry.

Throughout this period, the Coalition was stoutly defending its friends and financiers in the banks, and when Labor's 'Future of Financial Advice (FoFA)' legislation was finally passed in 2012, banning commissions and requiring advisers to act in the best interests of their clients, the Abbott-led Coalition promised to repeal it if it won government.

Under those new rules, financial advice did become more independent, but the problems didn't go away. Advisers were to be paid by their clients rather than the promoters of the products they were selling, but they were still selling, especially the ones employed by banks and AMP. People were more likely to get actual advice and not a sales pitch, but it was still too patchy. Crucially, the FoFA reforms required financial advisers to operate in the best interests of their clients – something we had all hoped, or even assumed, they were doing already.

The FoFA legislation was passed by parliament on 25 June 2012 and commenced on 1 July 2012. It introduced:

- a prospective ban on conflicted remuneration structures, including commissions and volume-based payments, in relation to distribution of and advice regarding a range of retail investment products
- a duty for financial advisers to act in the best interests of their clients, subject to a 'reasonable steps' caveat, and to place the best interests of their clients ahead of their own

when providing personal advice to retail clients. There is a 'safe harbour' provision with which providers can show they've met the best interests duty.

- an opt-in obligation that requires advice providers to renew their clients' agreement to ongoing fees every two years
- an annual fee-disclosure statement requirement
- enhanced powers for ASIC.

The FoFA reforms built on the *Financial Services Reform Act 2001*, which came into full effect in 2004. It regulated the education and training of financial planners, and established disclosure and compliance requirements: for example, financial planners had to disclose their fees and commission structures. Unlike FoFA, the FSRA rules did not state that planners had to act in their clients' best interests.

FoFA brought greater transparency and innovation and helped Australia inch closer towards a system in which financial planners were well qualified, their fees and charges were low and transparent, and they faced strong and binding incentives to act in investors' interests.

To my dismay and disgust, Tony Abbott remained stuck in the past. During the lead-up to the 2013 election, he campaigned against FoFA as a piece of Labor overregulation, and he reiterated his desire to repeal it. No wonder the Murray Inquiry didn't really tackle the issue when it was appointed by the Abbott government in 2013: the Coalition was still in Milton Friedman's deregulatory world of two decades earlier and, to be frank, they were also in bed with the banks. In some ways, the Coalition seemed to see itself as the political wing of the banks, as the ALP was the political wing of the union movement.

The Coalition and the banks remained in bed together until early 2018, when the full horror of what the industry had been up to started dribbling out in the royal commission – the one the Turnbull Coalition government reluctantly appointed when the banks themselves finally threw in the towel and asked for it. As the evidence mounted in 2018, the scales finally fell from the Coalition's collective eyes and (to mix some metaphors) they jumped out of bed and joined the rest of us on the other side of the road.

But back in December 2013 they were still in their 'save the banks from compliance burden' mindset, and they absurdly announced that the new fee disclosure requirements would only apply to new clients, along with a range of other measures that would have gutted FoFA. The storm of protest was swift and loud, and the attempt to neuter FoFA was blocked by the Senate. The conduct of advisers, and the interests of their clients, became the centre of a national political debate. But the debate was about to shift in a very important direction.

After a Senate committee chaired by Labor senator Mark Bishop called for a royal commission in mid-2014, the government went into full 'we don't need that' mode, and when ALP leader Bill Shorten formally made it part of the Opposition's policy platform in 2016, the government switched to an 'it will be a disaster' defence of the status quo. That stance lasted eighteen months, during which the government passed a series of measures, including the bank executive accountability regime, designed to demonstrate that a royal commission was not needed.

During this period, more and more stories kept coming out about financial planning scandals involving the banks, usually with the banks admitting fault, apologising and coughing up compensation. The final straw came when the Australian Transaction Reports and Analysis Centre nabbed the Commonwealth Bank for 53,506 breaches of the anti–money laundering laws, also admitted to by the bank, which ended up paying a fine of $700 million and all legal costs. From the moment that story emerged in August 2017, the argument about a royal commission was over.

'It is now in the national interest for the political uncertainty to end,' said the email from the banks to Malcolm Turnbull, suggesting he call a royal commission. 'It is hurting confidence in our financial services system, including in offshore markets, and has diminished trust and respect for our sector and people. It also risks undermining the critical perception that our banks are unquestionably strong ... We now ask you and your government to act to ensure a properly constituted inquiry into the financial services sector is established to put an end to the uncertainty and restore trust, respect and confidence.'

Oh dear. Was it hubris or a lack of awareness, or both? The banks had no idea what they were in for, and as a result nor did the government. Speaking after Turnbull announced the royal commission on 30 November 2017, Treasurer Scott Morrison said it was a 'regrettable but necessary action to take control', and overcome the damage to the financial system caused by all the calls for a royal commission.

As we now know, the tune of the government and the banks changed markedly after just a few days of public hearings at the royal commission. The stories that emerged were devastating.

3

The Conflict

THE ROYAL COMMISSIONER, KENNETH HAYNE, had only two jobs: first, to air the banks' dirty linen, and second, to lay out a path towards ending the conflicts of interest that caused the linen to get dirty. The rest was padding.

He did a magnificent job of his first task. Time after time during the commission, the basic flaw in the financial system was exposed by shocking, sometimes heart-rending, evidence from victims. They had trusted a financial adviser, only to find he or she had lost or wasted the money, through incompetence, or stolen the money, through fraud. Fees were extracted for no service, and in some cases no service was required because the client was dead.

The fundamental flaw – the conflict of interest that led to the vast majority of the misconduct uncovered by the royal commission – is that banks and wealth managers are allowed to own, employ and control financial advisers. They use them to sell financial products, so these advisers are not putting the client first, as customers are encouraged to believe. As in everything else, the payer of the piper calls the tune. Some banking misconduct revealed by the commission – such as the Commonwealth Bank allowing the use of its ATMs for money laundering, and undeserved bonuses for bank CEOs – didn't relate directly to the behaviour of in-house financial advisers. But almost all of the behaviour that caused ordinary people misery was a result of the central conflict of interest.

Hayne's task was simple and twofold: he had to expose the consequences of the conflict of interest at the heart of the financial system, and end it. He had to recommend that this set-up could not continue – that product and advice be separated. Nothing less would do, since all the laws, regulations and codes of conduct designed to 'manage' the conflicts had obviously failed – otherwise the royal commission wouldn't have been needed and there wouldn't have been so much dirty linen to air.

But in the second part of his task, he failed.

He said: 'I am not persuaded that it is necessary to mandate structural separation between product and advice.' Why not? Because: 'Enforced separation of product and advice would be a very large step to take. It would be both costly and disruptive.' Exactly! Disrupt away, I say. There needs to be some costly disruption, because the industry has been making too much money ripping people off.

In reaching his conclusion, Hayne said in his final report that he was persuaded by both the Australian Securities and Investments Commission and the Productivity Commission, which both recommended in their submissions that product and advice should not be forcibly separated. So the positions of those two government bodies deserve closer scrutiny.

The Productivity Commission's words were that 'forced structural separation is not likely to prove an effective regulatory response to competition concerns in the financial system'. 'Competition concerns' are the Productivity Commission's general brief. Its job is to worry about competition and efficiency, not so much the welfare of consumers. In recommending against structural separation of product and advice, the Productivity Commission was only talking about whether it was needed to enhance competition, which it's not. Competition is beside the point: the issue is not whether there is enough competition, or whether the industry is efficient enough, but whether people are getting ripped off.

ASIC's submission only suggested that structural separation should be delayed until more work was done on the extent and effect of conflicts of interest (as if we didn't already know enough about this). As part of its submission, ASIC talked about the review it had previously done of a random set of advice files, 'to test whether advice to switch to in-house products satisfied the best interests duty and related obligations under the Corporations Act'. They concluded: 'In 75 per cent of the advice files reviewed, the advisers did not demonstrate compliance with the duty to act in the best interests of their clients, including by "switching" clients from external to in-house products in circumstances where the pre-existing product appeared to be suitable'. So a staggering *three-quarters* of the files reviewed broke the law by not being in the best interests of the client. In the real world, anyone would see that scale of illegality as unbelievable and shocking, and would take dramatic steps to fix it. So what did the corporate watchdog do? Did it cancel all leave and launch the greatest crackdown on financial advisers Australia has ever seen? Not a bit of it. According to its royal commission submission, ASIC said it's 'working on a proposal ... to provide more transparency' and 'discussing with each of the licensees ... an appropriate response to its findings'.

ASIC was roundly castigated by Hayne, in his final report, for doing cosy deals with financial players. This seems to have produced a big change in ASIC's mindset on how urgently and robustly it responds to poor conduct. But the surprising thing is that ASIC's old view, produced under its former mindset (when it was in the business of doing cosy deals), seems to have influenced Hayne's decision on structural separation. He gave ASIC the rounds of the kitchen for being too soft on the industry, and yet he then listened to what it said, back when it was being too soft.

So Hayne stroked his elegant chin and came out with this: 'I observe ... that the Productivity Commission recommended, and I agree, that commencing in 2019, the Australian Competition and Consumer Commission (the ACCC) "should undertake 5 yearly market studies on the effect of vertical and horizontal integration in the financial system". The ACCC should study the impact of the conflict! Every five years!

Like the PC, the ACCC is concerned with competition. It also has a role in consumer protection, but not in the financial services industries – that was taken off the ACCC and given to ASIC. So that's what Mr Hayne decided to go with: no change to the structure of the industry, and a five-yearly review by an outfit not connected with consumer protection in financial services. To me this all sounds very slow, very soft and very odd.

Commissioner Hayne even seemed to argue against himself in the final report, with this statement near the start of it:

> The *Corporations Act 2001* and the *National Consumer Credit Protection Act 2009* speak of 'managing' conflicts of interest. But experience shows that conflicts between duty and interest can seldom be managed; self interest will almost always trump duty. The evidence given to the Commission showed how those who were acting for a client too often resolved conflicts between duty to the client, and the interests of the entity, adviser or intermediary, in favour of the interests of

the entity, adviser or intermediary and against the interests of the client. Those persons and entities obliged to pursue the best interests of clients or members too often sought to strike some compromise between the interests of clients or members and their own interests or the interests of a related third party (such as the person's employer, or the entity's owner). A 'good enough' outcome was pursued instead of the best interests of the relevant clients or members.

There was a second reason he chose not to recommend the forced separation of product and advice: that, in essence, the cost of compliance for financial advisers is so high that more banks and wealth managers are switching to cheaper straight-out sales anyway, instead of using 'advice-based distribution', as the companies put it.

As further changes to the regulation of the financial advice industry take effect over the coming years, those costs are likely to increase – or, at the least, are unlikely to reduce. It follows that the trend away from vertically integrated institutions may well continue, even if structural separation is not mandated.

At this point it's worth taking a small step back. The reason financial advice is so expensive – a financial plan usually costs around $3000, and advisers say they lose money on that, they just do it in the hope of picking up a long-term annual percentage fee – is because the compliance is so onerous. And the reason the compliance and regulatory demands are so onerous is because they are needed to offset the conflict of interest at the heart of the industry.

So while Mr Hayne relies on the rising cost of advice, he fails to address the obvious reason that it's happening: because the regulations and regulators are turning themselves inside out trying to deal with the lack of independence of financial planners, and the conflicts of interest inherent in product manufacturers employing people who call themselves advisers. But instead of actually dealing with that conflict and allowing the price of advice to eventually fall as result, he approvingly notes that the banks and investment companies are giving up on using advisers and just calling them salespeople instead.

They would probably be the same people, just called something different. I actually think that wouldn't be so bad – clients should know they are dealing with a salesperson, rather than an 'adviser'.

Unless separation between product and advice is mandated, the rules will always need to assume that conflicts exist, no matter how many firms drift away from vertical integration because using 'advice' to sell stuff is too expensive.

The fundamental problem is that because dealing with the conflicts of interest that are embedded in financial services has made the cost of financial advice prohibitive, the only way the system works is if the adviser is actually a salesperson on commission or charges a compounding percentage 'fee for service' over decades, so the lifetime value of the client is enormous. Needless to say, that means the lifetime cost to the client is also enormous.

Hayne was aware of this problem – in fact, he made a few recommendations to tighten the regulations designed to manage conflicts of interest. For example, Recommendation 2.2 says:

> The law should be amended to require that a financial adviser who would contravene section 923A of the Corporations Act by assuming or using any of the restricted words or expressions identified in section 923A(5) (including 'independent', 'impartial' and 'unbiased') must, before providing personal advice to a retail client, give to the client a written statement (in or to the effect of a form to be

prescribed) explaining simply and concisely why the adviser is not independent, impartial and unbiased.

On fees, he said:

The law should be amended to provide that ongoing fee arrangements (whenever made):

- must be renewed annually by the client;
- must record in writing each year the services that the client will be entitled to receive and the total of the fees that are to be charged; and
- may neither permit nor require payment of fees from any account held for or on behalf of the client except on the client's express written authority to the entity that conducts that account given at, or immediately after, the latest renewal of the ongoing fee arrangement.

And he also had some stuff to say about improving the quality of advice, mainly by reviewing the effectiveness of measures already taken by ASIC and the government, and also some measures to tighten up disciplinary procedures, including a requirement that all financial advisers should be individually registered. (At the moment, only the organisation they work at has to have an AFSL, or Australian financial services licence; the individuals are authorised representatives.)

That last bit is a good idea and could make a big difference. Individual registration, with the person answerable to a central disciplinary body, focuses the mind far more than simply working for a licensee, where it's up to the firm to discipline the person if he or she gets out of line. The problem with that system (the current one, that is) is that the best, most successful salespeople are often the loosest with the rules. Is the CEO of the advisory really going to sack the adviser who is shifting the most product and winning the most fee revenue? Of course not.

In a way, that gets to the heart of the issue: that banks and product firms have been motivated mainly by profit, rather than what's in the best interests of the client. Perhaps individual licensing of advisers as well as their employers will go some way towards dealing with that, but I think the best way to deal with it would be to only individually license them and not let them be employed by AFSL-holding product companies at all.

As Hayne himself said: 'Experience shows that conflicts between duty and interest can seldom be managed; self-interest will almost always trump duty.'

Or as Paul Keating once said, quoting Jack Lang: always back self-interest – at least you know it's trying.

Breaking brokers

Hayne recommended important changes to how mortgage brokers are paid:

> The borrower, not the lender, should pay the mortgage broker a fee for acting in connection with home lending.
>
> Changes in brokers' remuneration should be made over a period of two or three years, by first prohibiting lenders from paying trail commission to mortgage brokers in respect of new loans, then prohibiting lenders from paying other commissions to mortgage brokers.

It's interesting that the only part of the financial services sector that Hayne decided to be really tough on is also the subject of the only recommendation that neither political party is going to implement. He talked about not wanting to disrupt financial advice through structural separation of product and advice, but then recommended the ultimate disruption of mortgage broking. The royal commissioner was basically recommending the end of them. That's because no one – especially mortgage brokers themselves – thinks that borrowers will actually pay enough for the service.

At the moment, banks pay brokers a commission, both upfront and trailing, but Hayne said this is problematic because it gives rise to a conflict and unearned revenues: 'The present system of remunerating mortgage brokers is conflicted remuneration.' And: 'The chief value of trail commissions to the recipient, to put it bluntly, is that they are money for nothing.' It's hard to disagree with that, but the reason politicians have baulked at banning mortgage brokers' commissions is that, without those 'conflicted' commissions, mortgage brokers wouldn't exist, and about half the loans they write are from small lenders. In other words, they are a force for greater competition, because they genuinely give smaller lenders other than the big four banks a leg up. On the other hand, paying commissions for brokers to 'sell' loans is part of the reason Australia has such a high level of household debt, one of the highest in the world. The problem is that mortgage brokers represent the embodiment of marketed credit – the selling of loans   which has become an economic scourge.

Loans didn't used to be sold, they were applied for, and you got one if you were lucky. Household debt used to be around 30 per cent of GDP; now it's 120 per cent. That represents a significant threat to the nation's economic health, because it makes consumer spending fragile and extremely vulnerable to higher interest rates. It was only the corporate types who borrowed too much in the past, and in the 1980s they became fragile and vulnerable to higher interest rates and went down like nine pins when the Reserve Bank jacked up rates in 1989, causing the last recession this country has suffered.

The switch to seeing mortgages as a product to be marketed and sold like cars – with marketing strategies, advertising budgets and salespeople on commission – has led us, and the banks themselves, astray. Household debt really took off after 2000, when the banks took over wealth managers like BT, MLC and Colonial and learnt all about marketing and sales commissions. Marketed credit is why house prices went too high and became unaffordable for those, like my children, trying to get into the housing market, so the regulator had to step in and impose a credit squeeze. This is now having such a drastic effect on the housing market and is being transferred to the wider economy through a negative 'wealth effect' (simply that when consumers feel less wealthy they tend to save more and spend less). And marketed credit is one of the key reasons the banks lost their way. It fundamentally corrupted their sense of duty and risk, because it is simply not possible to maintain a sense of responsibility to customers – that is, to put the best interests of your client first – and to undertake careful risk assessments if you're desperately trying to sell something to them and earn a commission to feed your family.

In short, paying sales commissions for selling loans was a bad idea all round and should never have been allowed.

But Hayne isn't correct that mortgage brokers should be paid by borrowers, instead of lenders, for the simple reason that they won't do it and mortgage brokers wouldn't exist if they were forced to do it. The service isn't valuable enough for brokers to earn a living from it. Mortgage brokers do provide some value to borrowers: they help them shop around for the best rate and assist them with the loan application. But people won't pay $5000 cash for that, and that's the sort of money brokers need to make a living from it. It's what the banks pay them now, mostly in instalments over the life of the loan, calculated as a percentage. It's a difficult problem, perhaps the only real snag the royal commission has thrown up. Everyone agrees that mortgage brokers do a worthwhile job promoting small lenders and encouraging competition against the big four, so that without brokers they'd become much more dominant than they already are. But Hayne has also correctly highlighted the problems with the way brokers operate, in particular the commissions they're paid by banks. So someone needs to find a solution: how can the mortgage broking industry be kept alive to preserve competition, while ending conflicts inherent in commissions?

My suggestion is both simple and the only viable one: small lenders need to band together and set up an organisation that helps borrowers shop around and apply for loans among those small lenders, but with employees paid a salary, not commissions. It needs to be a separate, independent company that borrowers know will give them unbiased, unconflicted advice on where to get loans. It's a matter of evening the playing field and counteracting the marketing power of the big four banks: the Commonwealth Bank, Westpac, NAB and ANZ; the only way it can be done is by the competitors getting together and pooling their resources.

But in any case, it doesn't look like that's going to be needed, since both major political parties look like simply ignoring that Hayne recommendation and letting the banks continue paying commissions to mortgage brokers, perhaps only upfront commissions instead of the trailing commissions that Mr Hayne called 'money for nothing'. And as the chief of Australia's largest mortgage broking network told me: 'we don't care how they pay us, as long as it's the same amount of money'.

Will anything change?

Yes, of course, at least for a while.

Plenty has changed already, simply due to the banks' misconduct being exposed. Hayne did this well, and mercilessly. It was often gruesome to watch, and in many cases quite unfair; the evidence powers of the royal commission were used to skewer hapless witnesses who had just been following orders (always a weak excuse, of course). Many of those witnesses and/or their superiors ended up losing their jobs as a result: people like the chair of AMP, Catherine Brenner, and its CEO, Craig Meller, who both had to quit while apologising for the appalling scandals inside AMP that the commission unearthed quite early on, during some of the first public hearings. And then there were the chairman and CEO of NAB, Ken Henry and Andrew Thorburn, who were brutally dealt with in the final report by Hayne, singling out NAB:

> NAB also stands apart from the other three major banks. Having heard from both the CEO, Mr Thorburn, and the Chair, Dr Henry, I am not as confident as I would wish to be that the lessons of the past have been learned. More particularly, I was not persuaded that NAB is willing to accept the necessary responsibility for deciding, for itself, what is the right thing to do, and then having its staff act accordingly. I thought it telling that Dr Henry seemed unwilling to accept any criticism of how the board had dealt with some issues. I thought it telling that Mr Thorburn treated all issues of fees for no service as nothing more than carelessness combined with system deficiencies when the total amount to be repaid by NAB and NULIS on this account is likely to be more than $100 million. I thought it telling that in the very week that NAB's CEO and Chair were to give evidence before the Commission, one of its staff should be emailing bankers urging them to sell at least five mortgages each before Christmas. Overall, my fear – that there may be a wide gap between the public face NAB seeks to show and what it does in practice – remains.

That was devastating for NAB, and specifically for Henry and Thorburn; within a week, they were gone, forced out by a board of directors that had hanging over them an 88 per cent vote against the bank's remuneration at the 2018 annual general meeting. The rule with remuneration report votes is that two votes in a row of more than 25 per cent against means that there has to be a board spill and all directors have to stand for re-election. NAB directors knew that if they didn't get their act together and dump Ken Henry and Andrew Thorburn, they would be gone by the 2019 AGM.

That was the second time the NAB board had to sack both its chairman and CEO. The first was in 2004, when Charles Allen (chairman) and Frank Cicutto (CEO) both stood down following a foreign currency scandal in which some rogue traders lost $360 million and tried to cover it up. An investigation into the causes of that pointed the finger at NAB's dysfunctional culture and governance, which meant the top brass were goners. Of course, we can now conclude that NAB did not use those events in 2004 to fix its culture and governance, because they ended up having to do same thing again.

One large and telling difference between the 2004 and 2019 expulsions is that Frank Cicutto walked out with $13 million – that is, all the bonuses to which he might have become entitled – which would be worth about $25 million in today's money. Andrew Thorburn, on the other hand, only got six months' pay in lieu of notice, about $1 million, and none of the $22 million in incentive payments he might have been entitled to. You might think $1 million is still a lot of money, but for these guys it's peanuts. In some ways, that was the best indicator I've seen that Hayne had an impact: CEOs have always got big payouts when they are sacked, even when they have stuffed up, but if Thorburn's treatment is any sign, those days are gone.

Not long after the release of the royal commission's final report, both Matt Comyn, the new CEO of the Commonwealth Bank (the previous one, Ian Narev, was another of Hayne's victims), and Brian Hartzer, the CEO of Westpac, had to front up to a parliamentary committee review of the big four banks. They were contrition itself. Comyn said, 'It's been an extremely difficult and confronting process, which has identified a number of failures and issues where we've badly let down our customers and our broader stakeholders and we're very determined to fix that and to implement the substantial work.' Hartzer said something similar, although he also warned that cracking down on the banks too much might worsen the credit squeeze that small businesses and property investors were already suffering.

But remember this was a royal commission into *misconduct* in the financial services, banking and superannuation industries. It was never meant to be a general review of the structure of those industries like the ones led by Murray, Wallis, Martin and Campbell over the past forty years, or the previous royal commission into banking in 1937, which originally was meant to look into misconduct but ended up just being another academic review of the industry. We'll never know whether, when they inserted the word 'misconduct' into the name and terms of reference of this one, the Coalition government knew what they were letting themselves and the industry in for. But Hayne certainly took them at their word, as it were, and went for 'misconduct', big time. He zeroed in on it, making the public hearings a sort of carnival of complaint, a showcase of shenanigans.

And that will be the lasting impact of the 2018 royal commission, but it may not last all that long. History shows that unless structural issues are dealt with, people forget, or they leave and new people come along, and bad habits are reborn. If the structural conflict at the heart of financial advice is not dealt with by the government, because Hayne has specifically recommended against dealing with it, then it's inevitable that banks and wealth managers will slip back into their old ways before too long – that is, focusing on their own profits and personal incomes rather than the best interests of the clients.

That's why the rest of this book is designed to help you get some control over your money yourself, and why the book is called *It's Your Money* – because you can't really trust the industry that's meant to look after it for you. You should never fully trust others with your money anyway; you should always arm yourself with some knowledge. That doesn't mean you have to do it all your-self – you can't, just like you can't take out your own appendix or rewire your house. If you use a financial adviser or wealth man-ager, or even just have a superannuation fund, you have to hand your money over to them. So whether you like or not, you have to engage in an act of great trust, including letting them take their fees out of your funds, instead of sending you a bill the way a surgeon or electrician does.

That's why you need to know some stuff to protect yourself. The stuff about how we got to this point (Chapters 1 and 2), and what the royal commission did about it (Chapter 3), is important context and will help you understand the industry you're dealing with, but in the end *it's your money*.

EXECUTIVE PAY TENDS TO INCREASE WITH THE SIZE OF THE COMPANY

The bigger the company, the more the boss gets paid, even if he or she isn't working anywhere near as hard, or creating as much value, as the CEO of a smaller, less well-resourced business. Size matters, simply because with bigger businesses the executive salaries are a smaller and perhaps more defensible percentage of revenue. So CEOs tend to be keen to grow their businesses – and, where possible, make acquisitions. But the so-called 'four pillars' policy in Australia prevented the big bank CEOs from taking each other over (because banking had to consist of at least the four pillars – NAB, CBA, Westpac and ANZ) and they had already mopped up most of the smaller regional banks. That's another reason why Peter Smedley went on a takeover spree, and why David Murray bought Colonial and the others followed suit and bought life offices and wealth managers – it was the only way they could get bigger, and consequently considerably increase their salaries.

Shareholders are increasingly ready to reject mega salaries for bankers. Westpac's 2018 Remuneration Report ran to twenty-eight incomprehensible pages. The nub was that CEO Brian Hartzer received $6,572,180 in cash, STIs and LTIs. The report scored a 64.2 per cent vote against it at the Westpac annual meeting in December that year – a record high protest vote at the time. (The following week, NAB raised that inglorious bar with a vote against of more than 80 per cent.)

In other words, the tide has turned, in large part because of the Hayne Royal Commission, but fundamentally because of all the terrible stories of loss and corruption that led up to it. In response to a wave of community revulsion about what's been going on, bank boards – and boards everywhere, for that matter – are scrambling to adjust their thinking.

One after another, the bank chairs have had to face shareholders and tell them they have heard the message and promise to do better. Some have been more convincing than others, as shown by the protest votes mentioned above. Bonuses and salaries have been cut, but in some cases – specifically NAB and Westpac – not enough. The Commonwealth Bank didn't get a protest vote against the remuneration report in 2018 because executive bonuses were cut to zero; NAB CEO Andrew Thorburn received STI and LTI payments totalling $3 million, and Westpac CEO Brian Hartzer got bonuses totalling $3.6 million. Thus, protest votes.

2

YOUR
TOOLKIT

I F THE ROYAL COMMISSION MADE ONE THING CLEAR, it's that no one else will look after your money if you don't. To take control of your finances, you need to be familiar with some of the intricacies of the financial system – so you understand enough that a financial adviser can't bamboozle you. Knowledge is power.

My friend Paul Clitheroe is chairman of the Australian Government Financial Literacy Board and has actively campaigned about financial literacy for years, for which I really admire him. It's very worthwhile work, but financial literacy – having an understanding of the financial world – can only go so far. Most people still need advice. In my view, the point of financial literacy is to better arm you to deal with advisers. If it's all a complete mystery, you're vulnerable to being taken advantage of by charlatans and incompetents.

In this part of the book I arm you with the tools you need to successfully manage your finances in a post-Hayne world. Unfortunately, that world probably won't be all that different than it was before, but you are now much more aware of the fact that the financial and investing world is full of cons, crooks and careless characters.

It was a royal commission into misconduct, so it was always going to find and highlight the rip-off merchants in the sector. But the commission also highlighted some fundamental flaws in the structure of the industry and the way it's been regulated – and these aren't necessarily going to change. The regulators, ASIC and APRA, are going to be more active and tougher on the crooks when they catch them, but just because there are cops around doesn't mean you don't lock your door. You still take your own precautions.

In the following chapters, I give you the knowledge you need to protect yourself, so you know what questions to ask and can perhaps do some of the work yourself, if you want to. I guarantee that at the end of this book you will be sufficiently informed to be able to go forth and not get ripped off. You won't be qualified to set up shop as a financial adviser yourself, but you will be more confident in dealing with them, if you want to, and looking after your money yourself, if you want to do that.

I'm going to start with financial advice, because I think for most people it's the starting point, but also the most dangerous one. Most people need some form of advice, but this is also where most of the rip-offs occur. The financial advice industry is fraught with conflicts of interest and traps for the unwary, but that doesn't mean you should stay away from it. For most people, investing, and financial matters more broadly, is not their area of expertise. You might be a landscape gardener, a physiotherapist, a retail worker or a journalist: how can you be expected to know about investing? You can't.

Most advisers are decent, ethical people. The issue is not only that you need to know how to find a good one, but also that even the best advisers with the most integrity are battling an industry that is stacked against you. In my view, the greatest travesty of the financial world, laid bare by Commissioner Hayne, is that the financial industry can't be fully trusted. You need it, but you also need to be careful with it, and not naive. Read on ...

4

Getting Advice

I OFTEN COMPARE FINANCIAL PLANNERS TO DOCTORS. They are both professionals who help you stay healthy: one physically, the other financially. But there is one significant difference between them: the people who look after your financial health are much more expensive than those who look after your medical health, but they spend a lot less time training and preparing.

A visit to my doctor costs me $90 and takes about fifteen to twenty minutes, depending on what's wrong with me and whether he feels like a chat, and I get back $36.60 of that from Medicare, on the spot. Even if I need, or decide to have, a full check-up, I'm only up for a few hundred dollars for the pathology tests, and I get most of that back from Medicare.

But with a financial 'doctor', there's no option but to start with a full check-up, which can cost up to $5000, and there's definitely no financial Medicare to give you a refund. It might be free as part of an ongoing relationship, but that relationship could cost you many thousands of dollars per year for many years. Most financial planners don't send you an invoice – they take your money and invest it for you, and simply deduct their fee from the account, usually each quarter. Their fee is usually between 1 and 2 per cent: sometimes more when you include the full range of add-on costs that can sometimes get charged, and the amount is unregulated and disclosed only in private, often only in the fine print of long, unreadable documents. You can't compare it with a public list of typical fees. Your financial planner will keep an eye on your account, of course, and will come and see you once a year to go through it, but it's a fairly passive service, and the fee gets deducted month after month, year after year, no matter what.

If you have $1 million, an amount most retirees will end up with after a lifetime of super, the fee would be $10,000 to $20,000 per year, or $800 to $1200 a month. Compare it to a utility: how much do you pay for gas and electricity, which you use every day? And how much do you pay your doctor per year? You'd have to be pretty crook, and you'd have to be running your air conditioners day and night, to rack up $10,000, right? Yet that's how much financial 'health' will cost you.

And yet financial services are essential. Sure, perhaps not quite as essential as a doctor, or gas and electricity, but most people do need some level of financial advice, and if it were cheaper and more trustworthy more people would access it.

So here's my first bit of advice: negotiate the fee, and make sure the adviser tells you how much you will pay in dollars, not percentages, so you can understand it better.

A friend of mine told me recently that he has $3 million with an adviser who is charging him 1.3 per cent a year. 'Is that a lot?' he asked me. 'Am I getting ripped off?'

'Well,' I said, 'it's actually pretty good for the industry. You could be paying a lot more. But it's $39,000 a year – do you realise that?'

'Bloody hell! Thirty-nine thousand bucks a year! I had no idea!'

'Do you think what you're getting is worth that much?' I asked.

'Definitely not! But I like him and I think he's doing a good job. I just don't think he's worth $3000 dollars a month.'

'I agree,' I said. 'So you should talk to him.'

I saw my friend a few weeks later and asked him how it went.

'I went to see my adviser and told him that from now on I'd be paying him $10,000 a year, that's all.'

'How'd he take it?'

'He was fine, I mean, he grumbled a bit, but he's still looking after our money the same as he was.'

Which of course confirmed to my friend that, at 1.3 per cent, he'd been getting ripped off – in the nicest possible way, of course.

So if you're using an adviser already, here's what you should do: work out, in dollars, how much you are paying them and then consider whether you're getting good value. If you are – great. Don't change a thing. But I'm betting you're not, and the money the adviser is taking out of your account each year is the most you pay for any service and is more than you think it's worth. In this case, you should go see your adviser and discuss their fee – and get it down!

And then there are stories like those of Kevin and Barry.

When advice goes wrong

In the early 2000s, a Victorian father of two, Kevin Brown, attended a seminar organised by his accounting firm. Inspired by what he'd heard, he borrowed $250,000 to invest in what was claimed to be a tax-effective insurance bond scheme, with a 'guaranteed' return of 13 per cent per annum. (Several alarm bells here.)

After a year, his initial investment had shrunk to $235,000. Kevin's financial adviser explained that the decline was due to a tax payment. Then an investment bank contacted Kevin over concerns it had with the way the scheme was being managed. He withdrew the remaining funds. Two years later, the company running the scheme was wound up. Kevin was down $15,000 – and then he received a bill from the Australian Tax Office (ATO) seeking a further $50,000. The scheme, according to the ATO, was a deliberate loss-making venture. The hoped-for tax benefits were disallowed. Kevin's investment was a disaster.

Around the same time, Kevin also lost $26,000 in two other risky investments (a timber plantation and a gold mine). By now, he'd had enough of high-risk investments. He asked his financial adviser how to invest $50,000 in something that was safe and conservative. Based on these instructions and his adviser's guidance, Kevin's money was invested in a property development scheme run by the Perth-based Westpoint Corporation.

In New South Wales, Barry Hill also invested in Westpoint on the basis of advice from his financial planner. Having recently retired and sold his business, Barry was holding a lot of cash. His financial planner of twenty-five years advised him to invest $733,000 in four property developments. This included just over $480,000 in two Westpoint projects in Sydney and Melbourne.

The financial planner emphasised the investments' low level of risk. 'His exact words,' Barry said, 'were they were "safe as a bank".' Glossy marketing materials associated with the investments rated them as 'Triple A'.

'I repeatedly told him I wanted conservative investments,' Barry said. 'I was retiring and I didn't want to go into high-risk things. At our age, we don't want to risk everything. He kept telling me Westpoint was paying good interest, there were no charges and a good payout.'

In 2006, Kevin Brown's $50,000 disappeared in the $300 million collapse of the Westpoint Corporation. Barry Hill lost even more: nearly three-quarters of a million dollars in this and the other property investments that also failed. Thousands of other people who'd invested in Westpoint lost big: in many cases, their whole life savings.

Some of the investors had responded to press ads and seminars, but others had invested through licensed financial planners.

The reason these planners recommended Westpoint is simple: the company was paying a 10 per cent upfront commission. That is, for every $1 million invested in Westpoint – and there were quite a few million dollars – $100,000 went back to the planner.

In the process, the planners who recommended Westpoint committed nearly every sin in the book – because they didn't care. They were only interested in the commission.

They didn't understand the investment. Westpoint was a high-risk investment in property construction. Yet financial planners characterised it as low risk, 'like investing in a bank'.

They ignored the basic principles of asset allocation and diversification. Diversification across different investments and asset classes is critical to managing risk. Yet many investors put nearly all their capital into the one investment company, Westpoint, which represented one asset class, mezzanine finance – and a relatively obscure one at that. The ability to build appropriately diversified investment portfolios is a cornerstone of financial planning. Planners who led their clients to go 'all in' with Westpoint did not meet this key professional standard.

They failed to match the investment risk to their client's preferences. Some of the investors who sought low-risk investments were encouraged to borrow to invest in Westpoint. This borrowing had the effect of magnifying the risk of the already risky mezzanine debt product. Some of the investors staked their homes as security for their investment loans. And they lost those homes.

They weren't transparent about how they were being paid. Some customers received 'free' financial advice – which was actually paid for by the promoters of the scheme, and which turned out to be very expensive indeed. 'Free' financial advice (and 'free' real estate advice) should always sound alarm bells.

Overall, they didn't act in their clients' interests. This was perhaps the biggest sin of all. Planners put their clients into Westpoint because of the rich commissions and other benefits they received.

As a result of these sins, the financial planners caused immense damage to their profession and the wider industry. In the aftermath of the Westpoint collapse, and again after the GFC, angry and frustrated investors left their financial advisers in droves.

Much of what happened with Westpoint couldn't happen today – for example, those sorts of commissions are now banned – but the basic problem is still there: people serving themselves up to financial advisers and placing their trust where they shouldn't. The royal commission clearly showed that. So these events provide timeless lessons for how investors should use advisers and how they should approach investing.

When not to engage a financial planner

Not everyone needs a financial planner or adviser. If you are in your twenties or thirties, for example, and saving and contributing to super, you may not need an adviser: the simplest investment option – building as much super as you can in a good fund, taking a long-term view with a relatively high amount of investment risk – is probably best for you. You may be getting enough help and advice from your peers and your super fund. Financial advisers, like doctors, charge fees. And you don't go to the doctor just for the sake of it.

The picture changes, though, if you have special circumstances, such as too many debts, or an inheritance, or if you need help with budgeting. If you're struggling with debt or with budgeting, there are many sources of advice, including financial counsellors and the MoneySmart and mybudget.com.au websites. (Many councils and government agencies provide financial counselling services, as do some unions, charities and other associations.) There are also service providers such as Fox Symes, who, for a fee, will help you consolidate your debts.

And having your super in a good fund doesn't let you off the hook entirely. Being aware of how superannuation and the financial system work will help you get the best out of your super. What options should you choose within the fund? When should you choose them? How can you tell if your fund has gone from being good to bad? And what do you do about that?

In general, we should be able to let our finances tick away in the background so we can get on with enjoying our life, but it can't entirely be 'set and forget' – you need to keep an eye on your financial health just as you do your medical health. That doesn't necessarily mean you need a financial planner – at least not until you have enough assets to make it worthwhile.

What is a financial planner?

It's worth pausing for a moment to consider how the definition of a financial planner has evolved. The thing that has consistently struck me over the years about this profession is that there is a big difference between what financial planners' employees think they are, and how planners define themselves, and what the client thinks a financial planner is.

Before about 1980, anyone who needed financial advice went to their banker, accountant or insurance agent. As the market for investment and superannuation products started to grow about that time, the companies producing them needed a salesforce, so they started turning life insurance salesmen (they were usually men) into investment salesmen ... called financial planners.

It was a brilliant wheeze: we all knew that an insurance agent was a salesperson and approached them with appropriate caution. But a 'financial planner'? Why, that sounds like they're on our side.

As Commissioner Hayne pointed out in his interim report, 'most financial advisers came from a background of life insurance, in which a sales-driven, commission-based culture prevailed and comprehensive advice was not commonly sought or given. These being the roots of today's financial planning industry, the culture has endured.' Of course, not all financial planners were product salespeople, but the foundation and structure of the advice industry was about selling products. Indeed, for investment companies like AMP, the very definition of a financial planner was someone who distributed its products.

The regulation of advisers was also based on the notion that they were product distributors, especially until the Future of Financial Advice (FoFA) legislation in 2013, which banned sales commissions for financial advisers. Since then, the industry has focused much more on clients and providing actual advice, rather than being a sales service for investment product companies.

These days, a financial planner is, or should be, someone who can construct a financial plan – embodied in a Statement of Advice – and advise you on the complexities of the tax, pension and welfare systems, as well as financial markets. They should work alongside your accountant to make sure you are up to date with any changes in the superannuation system, and continually help keep you on track towards your financial goals, whether that involves saving or – after a lifetime of saving – living off your savings successfully.

What makes a good financial planner?

To invest successfully, you need to be careful who you listen to. Not all financial planners are the same. They vary in experience and education, in how they earn their income, and in whether they are licensed or not. A good financial planner:

- is licensed by the corporate regulator, ASIC
- has relevant specialist expertise, and preferably a degree qualification
- is able to offer the scope of services you need
- is committed to a high standard of probity and ethics, as expressed in a professional code or charter
- has a strong track record, and a clean one, as evidenced by references, good professional standing, and the absence of disciplinary action and litigation
- has access to good fund managers ('fundies')
- diversifies your investments between different assets and fund managers
- charges you transparently at a reasonable rate
- only charges you for actual, useful work.

You can check if an adviser is licensed (and whether they have been banned) via ASIC's MoneySmart website (moneysmart.gov.au).

Certified Financial Planner (CFP) is the highest designation a financial planner can hold. CFPs are qualified with a degree, have a set period of minimum professional experience, and adhere to the Financial Planning Association's (FPA) Code of Ethics and Rules of Professional Conduct. This code includes rules on disclosure, financial plan preparation and explanation, client service, complaints, education, competency and supervision. It can be viewed on the FPA's website (fpa.com.au). I recommend you only engage a planner who is a CFP or has an equivalent designation.

FPA members adopted Principles for Managing Conflicts of Interest to help members work in the interests of their clients. The principles include separately identifying financial planning fees in Statements of Advice, and regularly disclosing the total fees being charged.

STANDARDS FOR FINANCIAL PLANNERS

On 15 March 2017, the Corporations Amendment (*Professional Standards of Financial Advisers Act*) amended the *Corporations Act 2001* to raise the education, training and ethical standards of financial advisers. The *Professional Standards of Financial Planners Act* requires financial advisers who provide personal advice to retail clients on more complex financial products to hold a degree, undertake a professional year, pass an exam, undertake continuous professional development and comply with a code of ethics.

✓ **Tip:** It is best to use licensed financial planners, because they have clear responsibilities and there is recourse for investors if you do get into trouble.

✓ **Tip:** Choose an adviser with experience, but also one who is younger than you – to provide continuity later in life.

How to find a financial planner

When searching for a financial planner, it is often helpful to seek referrals from family and friends, and from any other advisers you have, such as accountants or solicitors. That only works, of course, if you or your friends or family already have professional advisers, or if you know people who know people in these fields. Many people don't. A friend recently said to me, 'I don't know a single person in my circle who has a financial planner, so word of mouth is not an option for me. I certainly don't have a solicitor. I have a tax accountant but, to be honest, I'm not really sure he's that great.' Fortunately, there are other options, including professional bodies and online resources. (Also, I advised my friend to get a new accountant!) There is a website called Adviser Ratings (www.adviserratings.com.au) that rates advisers and planners much like TripAdvisor does for accommodation and travel services. And several financial planning organisations and websites will help you find an adviser in your area:

- Financial Planning Association of Australia (fpa.com.au)
- Association of Financial Advisers (afa.asn.au)
- CPA Australia (cpaaustralia.com.au)
- Chartered Accountants Australia and New Zealand (charteredaccountants.com.au).

I wouldn't engage a financial planner unless he or she was a member in good standing with one of these bodies, and I would always check on Adviser Ratings to see how others rated them.

How to engage a financial planner

You should go about engaging a financial planner in the same way you would engage a gardener or a carpenter. Seek quotes from several different professionals, and interview them. Ask for references. And go into the relationship with your eyes open and with a sceptical frame of mind – you are recruiting someone you'll be working with for a long time, and who is very expensive.

An important part of engaging a planner is asking the right questions. A list of suggested questions is provided below. Use these, by all means, but also add your own questions. Before you meet with an adviser, spend some time thinking of questions that relate to your specific circumstances.

QUESTIONS TO ASK WHEN CHOOSING
A FINANCIAL PLANNER

Experience

- How long have you been in the advice business?
- Who have you mainly worked for?
- What are the most common sorts of clients that you advise?
- What are your clients mostly trying to achieve?

Qualifications and status

- What relevant training and qualifications do you have?
- Are you licensed?

Scope of services

- Do you take a special interest in a particular type of financial product?
- Are there any products that you do not recommend or give advice on? (This is important: you want to know if there are any asset classes not covered by the planner's advice, and you want to know if there are any products that the adviser steers away from, and why. Advisers are defined as much by what they say no to as by when and where they say yes.)

Approach

- How would you describe your style of advice?
- How do you approach financial planning?
- How do you go about understanding a new client?
- How do you deal with a client who may have conflicting objectives?

Fees

- What fees and other charges do you receive?
- What fees are you likely to charge?
- How do these fees work?
- How much is this advice likely to cost in dollars and as a percentage?

Professional development

- How do you keep up to date with changes in the industry?
- What training do you attend?
- Are you a member of any of the professional bodies?

Working with your financial planner

To get the best from your relationship with your planner, you should set clear ground rules for how you will work together: how often you will meet, and how you will communicate. And you should establish how the planner will be paid: my recommendation is that they should invoice a dollar amount, as opposed to you allowing the planner to take a percentage fee, but that may not suit you. There's nothing wrong with a percentage fee being clipped from your account, as long as you notice it! That is – you understand what it is, and more importantly how it is compounding.

You should also be clear about what you want to achieve; the planner can then use this information to analyse and evaluate where you are financially. The planner's analysis is then the basis for developing and presenting your financial plan.

Once you've understood and agreed to the plan, the planner will implement the plan's recommendations. After that, the relationship is about monitoring the plan and how it is working out.

A financial planner is legally obliged to give personal advice that suits your needs; to act efficiently, honestly and fairly; and to meet standards that are designed to protect you against anything going wrong. If needs be, you can always change the plan – and the relationship.

Inputs for your financial plan

The planner will ask personal and financial questions to understand your needs and goals. These are used to build a tailored investment strategy.

Once you have confidence in your planner, you should provide a clear and honest picture of your assets (what you own), liabilities (what you owe to others), income and expenses. When taking stock of your assets and liabilities, be careful not to leave anything out, including significant non-financial assets such as intellectual property, antiques and collectables. In cataloguing your debts, look closely at the loan terms as well as the different interest rates and other costs. With respect to your income and expenses, you should prepare a personal budget and share it with your planner.

✓ **Tip:** I'm often asked: if someone has personal debt, is investing still worthwhile? Paying off expensive debt first is best: it's the equivalent of earning a guaranteed, tax-free, high return.

INFORMATION FOR YOUR FINANCIAL PLANNER

- Personal details – basic details such as your age, family situation, employment details, contact details and so on
- Your current financial position: your assets and liabilities
- Information about your financial goals, such as when you would like to retire and what level of retirement income you would hope to have
- Information about your cash flow, such as how much you earn, how much you spend and what surplus is left for investment purposes
- Information about insurance and other protective buffers you may have in place in case something goes wrong. This includes levels of life insurance and your estate planning arrangements
- Information about your 'risk tolerance' or 'risk profile' and your investment time frame

✓ **Tip:** Not all debt is bad. For each of us at any point in our lives, there is an optimal level of debt. Think of debt as a tool for moving money across time. If you have high expected future earnings, and good ways to use money now, it pays to bring some of your future earnings into the present – by borrowing, but never too much.

APPOINTING AND WORKING WITH A FINANCIAL PLANNER: SUMMARY OF STEPS

First steps	Use your networks (if you can) and professional bodies to find nearby planners. Seek multiple quotes, and use the suggested questions on pages 86–7 to choose a planner well suited to your needs.
Contact the financial planning firm and ask for an initial appointment	Once you've selected a planner, meet with them and exchange information. The planner's firm will probably send you the Financial Services Guide, which outlines information about the planner and their services. Many firms also send out a client questionnaire at this stage for you to complete and return.
The first appointment	This is a chance for you to meet the planner and get a first impression of them. You should ask questions specific to your situation and ensure you are comfortable working with the planner – and that you are comfortable with the proposed fee. This meeting also gives the planner a chance to gather general information about you and your plans.

Preparation of the Statement of Advice	After the initial meeting, you let the financial planner know whether you want to go ahead with the financial planning relationship, such as by signing a letter of engagement. After you have done this, the planner will prepare a Statement of Advice and the paperwork that helps with the implementation of advice, including the Product Disclosure Statements and application forms. It can take some time for a Statement of Advice to be written. Agree on a time frame before this process starts so you know what to expect.
Statement of Advice presentation	The planner presents the Statement of Advice along with other documents needed to implement the financial plan.
Implementation	This is an essential part of the financial planning process: putting the recommendations into practice.
Ongoing relationship	Ongoing financial planning support may range from six-monthly reviews (if you have a large portfolio) through to ad hoc reviews as and when you need them. It is important to understand upfront the level of ongoing service you need and will receive, and what ongoing fees you will pay. You should advise your planner when your circumstances change, and you should review the relationship with your planner regularly. Remember, you are in charge. It's your money!

STATEMENT OF ADVICE

Section 947B of the *Corporations Act 2001* summarises the key components that are required in a Statement of Advice. These include:

- a statement setting out the advice – what the financial planner is advising you to do
- the basis of the advice – why it is suitable given your needs; how it will help you to meet your financial goals
- information about how the financial planner is getting paid and all other fees associated with the Statement of Advice (such as managed fund fees, administration fees and insurance premiums)
- details about anything that might influence the financial planner's advice (for example, them holding shares in the company of a fund manager they are recommending)
- any relationship the financial planner might have that could influence the advice.

What to do when things go wrong?

In the Westpoint example earlier in this chapter you saw several ways in which the planner relationship can go wrong. It's usually because the planner is not putting your interests first, because he or she is earning a commission for selling you something. The days of this happening should be over. But there still might be conflicting interests, the planner might lack key skills, or their advice might be plain wrong. The Hayne Royal Commission revealed multiple examples of planners delivering unsuitable advice. Another example is given in the following case study.

Case study: Suitability of advice

Based on advice from his financial planner, Ben Mackenzie invested in a vineyard as a way to earn money and minimise tax. By the third year, according to projections, the vineyard's operating costs would be recovered through the sale of grapes and bottled or bulk wine. However, prospectus forecasts were not met, largely as a result of a drought, but also because mass vine plantings created a wine glut and prices dropped.

In accordance with the licence deed, the project manager requested additional funds from the investors to maintain the vineyard's viability. Ben had invested a total of $55,900 in the project and decided against contributing further capital.

Those investors who did make additional payments converted their entitlement into shares when the scheme became an unlisted public company. Ben, though, lost his entire investment.

He believed he'd not been made aware of the structure and nature of the investment or the risks involved. He did not expect to be asked to make additional payments in the long term.

The Financial Industry Complaints Service panel found the financial adviser had not breached his duty of care because his client understood the nature of the investment and the risks involved.

But the panel ruled that there was a shortfall in the financial adviser's performance, because he should have kept Ben informed of the vineyard's financial decline. It ruled: 'He had no expectation that he might have to prop up the investment long term and when he continued to receive bills he was not offered any advice or assistance on what his options were.'

As a result, the panel ordered the financial planner to refund the commission he received on the vineyard investment, plus interest. (But not the whole investment, mind, that was gone – just the commission.)

Be on the alert for bad advice. This means informing yourself as much as you can, and trusting your instincts. Listen to the niggly voice inside that says 'this sounds fishy' or 'is this too good to be true?' Commercial incentives and conflicts of interest in the financial services industry generate a fog of bogus insights and pseudo-wisdom – most of it unhelpful for investors, and self-serving for advisers.

Learn from the lessons of the Westpoint investors and the royal commission, and poor Ben: those lessons were expensive, and invaluable.

If you do receive poor service from your financial planner, you should complain – to the professional association, the regulator ASIC, or the Financial Ombudsman Service, depending on the nature of your complaint. This is important for you, obviously, but also for others. Accurate feedback about performance makes the whole system work better. So rate your adviser, give feedback, complain, and escalate the situation if you feel you should.

If things aren't working out, or if you lack confidence in your financial planner, you can always change to another one.

If things get really tough, the law society or law institute in your home state will offer a referral service or directory for finding a solicitor or barrister.

Fees, fees, fees

Unfortunately, the end of advisers charging commissions was not the end of problems with fees. Instead of commissions, advisers started charging on a 'fee for service' basis. This is a small step in the right direction – there is less of a conflict of interest – but there are still plenty of pitfalls for investors, mainly that the fees were still usually a percentage of your money, deducted every year. The level of fees was and is high, and the way they are charged is not at all clear. Investors were often getting a bad deal and, crucially, they weren't in a position to control their investments.

Over the past few decades, just as a rich garden of new investment options has sprung up, so too an incredible diversity of fees and charges has been foisted on us. Management fees, performance fees, transaction fees, advice fees, establishment fees, admin fees, master-trust fees, shelf-space fees, upfront commissions, trailing commissions, entry and exit fees – almost always a percentage. This proliferation of percentage fees is not in investors' interests.

That's because the impact of a percentage deduction from your account acts like compound interest – it gets bigger and bigger as time goes on.

Business Magnate Warren Buffett explained this better than I can in his 2019 letter to the shareholders of Berkshire Hathaway, talking about his first investment – $114.75 at the age of eleven, in 1942.

If my $114.75 had been invested in a no-fee S&P 500 index fund, and all dividends had been reinvested, my stake would have grown to be worth (pre-taxes) $606,811 on January 31, 2019 (the latest data available before the printing of this letter). That is a gain of *5,288 for 1*. Meanwhile, a $1 million investment by a tax-free institution of that time – say, a pension fund or college endowment – would have grown to about $5.3 *billion*.

Let me add one additional calculation that I believe will shock you: If that hypothetical institution had paid only *1%* of assets annually to various 'helpers,' such as investment managers and consultants, its gain would have been *cut in half*, to $2.65 billion. That's what happens over 77 years when the 11.8% annual return actually achieved by the S&P 500 is recalculated at a 10.8% rate.

The industry has an uncanny ability to find new ways to extract money. It also has a lot of front when it comes to setting high commissions. Some commissions – such as those for Westpoint and managed investment schemes like timber plantations – were as high as 10 per cent of the clients' funds! So with $100,000 invested, you were actually investing $90,000. The $10,000 difference, from your point of view, was gone forever. Happily, those sorts of fees are also gone forever.

After the introduction of compulsory superannuation, the value of funds under management grew rapidly – and so did the level of fees being earned by financial planners and fund managers. In fact, they grew much faster than inflation, and much faster than the rate of growth in the economy as a whole. To achieve this growth, the industry had to … well, they didn't have to do much at all.

I have long argued that a few basic principles should guide how investors should be charged. Fees should be clear, they should be reasonable, and they should be directly matched to the provision of services that investors want and need. These principles are sacrosanct. They should be the basis for how financial advice is sold.

However, the financial services industry has not held to these principles. Instead, there is a big disconnect between fees and services. Many of the fees being charged look like gouging. At a time when financial advisers' costs have been falling, fees have stayed high. Investors, it seems, are again being ripped off.

The proliferation of fees can be a silent disaster for investors. Layer upon layer of percentage fees can compound to a level that squashes your returns. A moderate-sounding management fee plus a moderate-sounding platform fee plus a modest fee for your adviser – together these can add up to something that is very far from moderate.

Percentage fees in particular can erode your savings at a cracking pace. Suppose you have a balanced portfolio that is earning

9.8 per cent. A 2 per cent fee would knock out more than one-fifth of your total return. This is truly awful, as is the allocation of risk: you have much more at stake than your adviser does. Percentage-based fees are often terrible for you, but they are a boon for the financial services industry.

Percentage-based fees can make it difficult for investors to grasp the actual dollar amount being charged. A 2 per cent fee on a portfolio of $100,000 might not sound unreasonable, but a $2000 cash fee would seem very significant indeed if you got an invoice for that amount. For this reason, in my career I've pushed for time-based service fees to replace percentage fees levied on the size of a client's portfolio.

Hourly rate fee-for-service charging has the advantage that compensation for the financial planner is closely tied to the work they do, not just 'skimming' a fee off your capital. Many other professions – such as accountants and lawyers – rely on hourly rate fees.

For a long time, I've been saying that the percentage fees for *all* financial services – not just financial planning and funds management – are too high and that they are bleeding our retirement savings.

Investing is a constant battle against hidden fees, higher taxes, rising inflation, baffling jargon, self-serving claims and complicated investment products. It is a 'game of inches': shaving your fees and charges down just a few points can make a huge difference to your end result. Excessive fees are more important than the difference between a good and a middling fund, for example. Your fees (as well as tax effectiveness and other sources of value leakage) are much more controllable than the vagaries of markets and the relative performance of different asset classes and sectors.

The problem with investment and advice fees is that there is no regulation of them, no standardisation, no reliable comparison data, no guidance and not much disclosure of them. Fees are generally charged as a percentage of your total sum – not by the hour, like lawyers and accountants. The percentage for advice is usually somewhere around 1 per cent, but it could be more or less than that. Some advisers do charge by the hour, or a fixed amount of dollars as a monthly retainer, but they are few and far between. They love percentages because it doesn't sound like much money.

One per cent? That doesn't sound like much. But if you've got a million dollars – and most people do when they retire with their super lump sum – that's $10,000 per year. And don't forget, they're not sending you a bill for that amount, they're just taking it from your account periodically, and the period, by the way, is up to them.

The other problem is that you're usually not charged one fee. There's the advice fee, then the fund manager fee, the administration platform fee and the custodian fee. Usually you're lucky to get out of it for less than 2 per cent ... ka-ching! That's $20,000 a year.

And finally, percentage fees compound – that is, they get bigger and bigger as time goes on: just by doing nothing, investments tend to grow at around 6 to 8 per cent a year, which means the fee is increasing by that as well, without them having to ask for an increase. It just happens.

If your financial adviser, fund manager or stockbroker is not helping you squeeze all you can from your investments, you need to find someone who will. Ask yourself each year: when was the last time I spoke to my advisers about getting my fees down? When did I discuss the fees at all?

So when considering an investment, don't just focus on the stated return. Also keep your eye on risk and capital protection, and on fees, which come in many different forms.

Quality of advice

Let's return to the health–wealth comparison. Both are essential to long-term happiness. Doctors are to your health what financial planners should be to your wealth. And yet there are stark differences in how doctors and financial planners are trained, regulated and paid. These differences have led to serious problems in the quality and value of financial services.

Doctors train for a minimum of six years at university and in hospitals. Many different controls are in place to make sure you receive quality medical care, and that you receive good value. When you visit your doctor, you might pay a fee of less than $100, and you usually receive a government rebate. When it comes to routine health questions, the value for money you receive is usually very good.

(Not all doctors are saints, mind you: a 2018 *Four Corners* episode blew the whistle on gouging by some specialist surgeons. The lesson is that you should shop around, even when it's for an obstetrician or an orthopaedic surgeon. After all, it's your body!)

With financial advice, however, the value-for-money equation is different. If you hand over $1 million to an adviser, he or she might charge you a 1 per cent fee; that's almost $1000 per month! And from month to month, your financial adviser will do very little. Usually you get a once-a-year consultation and check-up.

Despite the fact that they are entrusted with the importance of managing all your savings, financial planners have been able to offer services with few skills and little oversight. While some planners are experienced and well qualified, others entered the market after only minimal training. The least qualified advisers were given a ticket to work after completing only a short diploma course.

In 2007, for example, it was possible to do an eight-day, exam-free course and become a financial planner equipped with a 'Diploma of Financial Services'. Following a further eight-day course, planners could step up to an 'Advanced Diploma of Financial Services'. (This spoke volumes about not only the state of the financial system but also the state of our vocational training system.)

As with the former life insurance reps, much of the training of planners involved learning about the products for sale, rather than how markets work, how wealth is created, or the ethics of finance and investment. Even today, despite the *Professional Standards of Financial Advisers Act*, a large number of financial planners do not have a degree qualification.

Investors who met with financial planners walked away with a pile of paperwork but considerably less insight. This situation was not entirely the fault of advisers or their industry. Under the FSRA, financial planners had to demonstrate adherence to 'know your client' and 'know your product' rules. These meant financial planners had to know and understand their clients' needs and match them with the most suitable products.

In an important respect, the FSRA emphasis on disclosure was counterproductive. Transparency was hard to achieve amid a fog of documents. Altogether, the statutory Statement of Advice, the Financial Services Guide and the Product Disclosure Statement often ran to hundreds of pages. Few clients were willing to plough through it all. In more than one way, the system of advice wasn't serving investors' interests.

STRUCTURAL CORRUPTION

The first ASIC survey of financial planning, conducted in 2003 with the Australian Consumers' Association (ACA), found the industry to be 'structurally corrupt'. Of the 124 financial plans issued to the sixty shadow shoppers participating in the survey, only two were regarded by a panel of experts as 'very good'. Only 29 per cent were regarded as 'OK', and 51 per cent were assessed as borderline, poor or very poor. Planners' shortcomings were serious, including not following the law and providing unsuitable advice.

These findings were backed up by other ACA surveys and by subsequent ASIC investigations. A 2006 ASIC surveillance campaign that focused on superannuation switching reached a devastating conclusion: 16 per cent of the advice was not reasonable, given the client's needs. In other words, investors had a one in six chance of receiving bad advice. Other findings included:

- When clients were advised to switch funds, a third of the time it was without credible reasons and had the potential to leave the client worse off.
- Unreasonable advice was three to six times more common when the adviser had an actual conflict of interest over remuneration or product recommendations.
- Consumers found it difficult to detect bad advice.

In 46 per cent of cases, advisers failed to issue a Statement of Advice, the mandatory written statement of the advice given and the reasons why.

Similar findings came to light at the royal commission. No one should have been surprised at what Commissioner Hayne and his team uncovered.

The company behind the brand

One particular challenge for consumers is understanding the network of relationships between financial planning businesses – or 'dealer groups' as they are called – their owners and related financial products. These ownership relationships are usually disclosed somewhere, but often not prominently. In the wake of the royal commission, relationships between large financial services institutions and financial planning firms and fund managers are a major concern for investors and regulators – and the relationships are very much in flux, as many banks and wealth managers are exiting the markets for financial advice. As always, you should ask questions and do your homework about who owns whom, and whose interests are front of mind for your adviser.

Computerised financial advice, aka 'robo-advice'

In addition to traditional 'analogue' sources of financial advice, there are also 'digital' sources. Aspects of the financial advice process can be automated. So-called 'robo-advisers', such as Betterment and Wealthfront, provide digital advice services online and through smartphone apps.

Most robo-advice is 'free' – so long as you invest your money with the firm providing it. That is, it's the way they help you choose how to allocate money to their various funds. You then pay a percentage of your money each year to the fund manager.

As a generalisation, it's fair to say you get what you pay for, but while human advice is too expensive, robo-advice could be described as too cheap. It's just a machine giving you an asset allocation formula according to the various inputs you enter. It doesn't cost the provider a thing, but it could end up costing you a lot if your investment returns are sub-par.

When you register with a robo-adviser website, you answer questions about your income and expenses, assets and liabilities, goals, objectives and risk appetite. A computer algorithm then uses this information to make recommendations. People with similar investment objectives receive the same advice. Robo-advisers charge lower advice fees, and most of the time no advice fee at all. But you do pay when ultimately you follow the advice and end up investing with them. A fee may be charged on a fee-for-service basis, or as a percentage of assets under management. You may also be charged a subscription fee for ongoing services.

But what do you lose by not having a human adviser? Unlike a flesh-and-blood financial planner, a computer program cannot ask probing questions designed to dig deeper into your attitudes to risk – a central element when designing an appropriate investment strategy – and certainly can't deal with specific issues you might have with estate planning, budgeting or tax. In the FPA's submission to the Productivity Commission's inquiry into superannuation, it supported ASIC's view that human beings should be involved in the provision of financial advice:

Financial services firms deploying algorithms need to make sure their logic is explicable to customers and regulators and that a human being is made responsible for any problems that might emerge with the code ... The pace of innovation is speeding up and that means that products and services – including financial products – are being delivered using technology often with little or no involvement of human beings ... ASIC don't want to see algorithms shifting the risk to consumers or others in society ... For an algorithmic system there must be a person who is responsible for its design and its outcomes ... Given the limited understanding of how software makes decisions, automated decisions must be transparent and explained.

Robo-advice services are usually limited in their scope; for example, typically they do not consider whether your money would be better used for other purposes, such as paying down debt. They will not clarify your investment goals and objectives, or make tailored adjustments if your investing is not going to plan. If you enter incorrect information, the computer won't know, and could give you the wrong advice. It is common for robo-advisers to emphasise certain types of investment (such as exchange-traded funds), rather than the full range of investment alternatives.

✓ **Tip:** Robo-advice may be more suitable if you don't want (or can't afford) full-service financial advice, or if you have simple advice needs or only a small amount to invest.

Robo-advice definitely has a place, but it should be treated as simply a tool, just like the calculators available at ASIC's MoneySmart consumer website.

Conclusion

I know a lot of terrific financial advisers – in fact, I haven't met many bad ones – and I know that it's not only possible to have a productive and respectful relationship with one but also essential for anyone who has a bit of money to invest. If you're starting out, then you're fine with a super fund, letting it grow, but if you're older and have the challenge of getting the most from a lump of capital without losing it, then you need an adviser.

I hope you come away from this chapter, and this book, better armed to have that productive and respectful relationship, where you're clear about what you expect, and able to ask the right questions.

5

Basic Principles

EVERYONE SHOULD UNDERSTAND AT LEAST the basics of investing – even if you have only a modest amount of money, and especially if you have a lot of debt.

Making the best use of your assets and liabilities means making your money work for you – in other words, investing it. In some ways, the most important part of investing is preserving your money, what Warren Buffett called Rule No. 1 – 'Don't lose money' (and Rule No. 2 was 'Remember Rule No. 1'). But apart from being a way to *preserve* your money, investing is a way to *grow* it.

Running a business is 5 per cent ideas and plans, and 95 per cent sweat. Investing is the same. It's a long game, one that requires patience and discipline. Slow investing usually wins the race; fast investing is gambling, which can sometimes win, but the odds are stacked against you.

Compound interest

To be a smart investor, there are some fundamentals that you need to be familiar with. They aren't complex, but they are essential to making the very best of your money. The first and most important of these is compound interest, the power behind superannuation.

Compounding a particularly high return (of, say, 20 to 25 per cent per annum) by reinvesting interest and dividends is the difference between wealth and extreme wealth. This level of compounding is the basis for the fortune of Warren Buffett, and that of 'Australia's Warren Buffett', Alex Waislitz. If they'd been compounding at 8 or 10 per cent over the past few decades, they'd still be doing okay, but we probably wouldn't know their names, and I wouldn't be writing about them in this book.

> *Over the 63 years [from 1926 to 1988] the general*
> *market delivered just under a 10 per cent annual return,*
> *including dividends. That means $1000 would have*
> *grown to $405,000 if all income had been reinvested.*
> *A 20 per cent rate of return, however, would have*
> *produced $97 million.*
>
> WARREN BUFFETT

Compound interest underlines why it is so critically important to care about every percentage point, including percentage fees imposed by financial planners and fund managers.

> *For a 21-year-old on a starting salary of $50,000, the*
> *difference between a 5 per cent return and a 6 per cent*
> *return translates into a 23 per cent difference in*
> *retirement savings, a nominal difference of $255,000*
> *or five years' pay.*
>
> PRODUCTIVITY COMMISSION

And just remember: that 1 per cent difference is probably the fee.

Investment returns come in two forms: capital gains (or losses), and income – in the form of interest, dividends or rent. You make a capital gain when you sell an investment for more than you paid for it.

Capital value at any time is basically a calculation of its future potential to earn income: that is, in theory someone will only pay for an asset an amount that equates to the present value of what they think it will earn for them in future. So a capital gain comes about because the buyer thinks it will earn more income in future.

Of course, it's also true that people speculate, rather than invest, which means, in essence, that they hope to sell it to another speculator who buys with the intention of selling to another speculator, and so on. That's sometimes called 'pass the parcel'.

Capital gains tend to receive more attention in the media and among financial commentators: everyone loves the story of a stock market boom – or a meltdown, unless they're in the middle of it. But both capital gains and income are important. The total return on your investment is the sum of all the income you earn and the net capital gains you make.

The 'yield' on any asset is the return you can expect to receive, expressed as a percentage per annum of the asset's purchase price.

Risk

'Risk' is often misdefined and misunderstood. There are many different types of risk. People speak of market risks, inflation risk, tax deductibility risk, country risk, sector risk, sovereign risk, delivery risk, fulfilment risk and a plethora of other risks. (Perversely – even though a long life is generally regarded as a good thing – the risk of a person outliving their savings is referred to as 'longevity risk'.)

When an investment professional – that is, that is someone who is in the business of investing other people's money – talks about risk, they usually mean volatility. A super fund especially doesn't want too much of that, because they have people retiring all the time, and it's not fair if someone cashes in their chips when values happen to be low. Also, investment managers are measured every quarter, and it doesn't look good to have wild swings in their quarterly returns.

For someone saving for retirement over the long term, risk means something different. Fundamentally, it's about the end result: that is, the extent to which returns will be delivered as promised, and the extent to which your initial investment is safe and doesn't get lost. Insofar as reliability is about volatility – the extent to which returns move up and down – investors are most concerned with 'downside volatility', which is an overcomplicated way of saying whether or not you will lose your shirt. Sharply negative returns can deplete your capital, or destroy it altogether.

Understanding risk is crucial to success in investing. A common problem in risk management is that people focus on the wrong types and sizes of risk. People in financial markets spend a long time worrying about the next financial crash, or the next big corporate collapse, for example, but pay less attention to the small mistakes and insidious leakages that can erode the rate of return and the value of your investments. We are wrong not to focus on these other costs, because, unlike the first ones, they are not rare or uncertain; they can happen all the time and – unless actively guarded against and purged – they happen with certainty.

The risk–return trade-off

Risk has a value. Investors who take on the possibility of negative returns need to be compensated. Consider two returns that have an expected payoff of $100 per year. Investment A will yield $100 per year with certainty. Investment B is expected to yield $100 on average, but in some years will generate more and in some years less. In order for investors to be willing to hold investment B, they must be compensated, so they have to be able to buy investment B at a lower price than investment A, and therefore achieve a higher expected return.

This is an example of the 'risk–return trade-off'. The greater the risk, the greater the expected return. The idea that you should be paid for taking risk with your money is fundamental to investing. In principle, the more risk you take, the more you should be paid, or at least the higher the return you should expect.

And most importantly, the converse applies: the higher the return, the higher the risk is likely to be. Another way of putting that is: there's no such thing as a free lunch. Another cliché: 'if it seems too good to be true, it probably is'.

That's not to say you shouldn't take risk. In fact, it's really the only way to get a decent return, especially these days. The whole idea of investing is to take some risk to get a better return than if you'd just put the money in the bank. The important thing is to understand the risk you're taking, and to do it with your eyes wide open.

There are few certainties in investing, but here is one: if anyone tells you they've broken out of the risk–return trade-off, enabling them to earn reliably high returns at a low risk, they are lying, or delusional. Investors caught up in the Westpoint collapse were receiving a 12 to 13 per cent 'guaranteed' yield – except they most definitely were not.

Risk should be seen as a measure of the reliability of your investment returns. This includes the safety of your original investment. If your returns are unreliable, you need to be compensated for this. That is the basis for the risk–return trade-off.

Over long time frames, high-risk assets – such as start-ups, some shares and property, and some foreign and exotic securities – produce the highest returns. While there are rewards for accepting some level of risk, the challenge is to make sure that the risks you take are calculated ones, and that you are being compensated for taking them.

Risk appetite

Understanding your willingness to take risks – in other words, your 'risk appetite' – is critical to investing. It's a major driver of the type of investments you should select; and it's therefore something your financial adviser should ascertain carefully: how well they do that is a good measure of whether they're up to the job. Some investments involve very high levels of risk, and they are suitable only for investors with a high risk appetite. Mismatched risk can be a shock. The royal commission heard multiple examples of what can go wrong if the risk of an investment doesn't match the investor's risk preferences and appetite.

QUESTIONS TO ASK YOURSELF ABOUT RISK APPETITE

- What are you investing for? Are you hoping to preserve or grow your investment amount?
- When do you expect to need to call on your investments? If you are unlikely to need to call on your investment for a long time, then a low return is probably not suitable.
- Are you someone who is comfortable with a higher level of risk? Would you, for example, be prepared to chance losing most or all of the value of your investment, in exchange for a higher expected return? Do you relish the daily drama of financial markets?
- Are you a worrier? Remember that losing your money in a high-risk investment is not the only thing to worry about. If you only invest in low-risk investment products, your money might grow too slowly, and it might be eroded by inflation and tax. There are many different kinds of investment losses, some more visible than others.

RISK TOLERANCE: AN EXAMPLE

In the last thirty years, Australian share returns have averaged about 15 per cent, but the biggest one-year fall was almost 40 per cent. That means that someone with $1 million invested could have $400,000 at risk in any one year. It's a frightening thought, especially for someone who is close to retirement. Another example: Australian listed property fell 55 per cent in 2008 – a similar catastrophe would wipe out more than half your portfolio, which would take years to recoup.

Investor psychology

Some brave scholars have tried to study the psychology of investors' decision-making. Nobel laureate Daniel Kahneman developed 'prospect theory' with Amos Tversky. In hundreds of experiments, Kahneman and Tversky compared how people felt about losing $100 with how they felt after winning $100.

Most people, it turns out, are 'loss-averse': they feel more pain from a loss than joy from an equivalent gain. They also prefer a smaller, certain gain over a larger, uncertain one. This phenomenon can be observed in many real-world markets, such as when, after a market crash, investors buy stocks that offer regular dividend payments rather than stocks that have big potential for capital gains. By seeming to 'play it safe' in this way, investors actually curtail their future returns.

Psychology can affect investment in other ways, too, such as how frequently people buy and sell securities. Professor Terrance Odean, for example, found that overconfident investors traded so frequently that they undermined their returns (due to brokerage and other costs). Specifically, over the period he studied, frequent traders earned a net annual return of 11 per cent while infrequent traders earned a return of 19 per cent.

Investing is about people. I really hate the term 'equities' for shares in companies, as if it's some disembodied asset. You don't ever really just invest in an 'asset'; you invest in people. No matter how large a bank or a corporation is, its performance is all about the people who work there or worked there in the past. Integrity and expertise are therefore crucial.

When buying shares, don't invest according to a label like 'value investing' or 'growth investing' – those sorts of terms are convenient for professionals, but don't mean much to ordinary investors. If you're investing in companies, look for ones that are well run, ethically minded and in growing industries, and that have good ideas.

'Everything in moderation' is a good principle. The most common causes of investment underperformance usually involve some kind of excess: excessive diversification, excessive concentration, too much liquidity, not enough liquidity, excessive fees and, yes, paying too much for advice and help.

Case study: Capital protection and risk tolerance

Rose Chan was faced with having to decide what to do with the proceeds of her late son's estate. On the advice of a financial planner, she invested in a shares fund.

Rose said she wanted to safeguard her son's estate and that security of the investment was more important to her than wealth creation.

The financial adviser drew up an executive summary, which stated: 'Our recommendations will enable you to achieve the following: Minimise your tax liabilities; Ensure your capital does not diminish early in retirement and your income increases with inflation; Enjoy your lifestyle without being concerned with your financial affairs; Be organised and in control of your financial affairs; Structure your cash flow so it is received on a regular basis.'

The summary went on to say that a minimum return of 6 per cent was achievable and that little or no tax would be paid each year.

Over twelve months, Rose put $410,000 into a shares fund, including $200,000 from the sale of a property.

The investment product established by her adviser had a 29 per cent weighting to international shares, 13 per cent Australian shares, 6 per cent Australian property securities, 2 per cent international property and infrastructure, and 5 per cent to private equity.

Less than halfway into the investment timeline, Rose decided to take her money out, thereby crystallising a $102,135 loss. In her formal complaint about the loss, she said the potential volatility of the investment had never been explained to her. 'The adviser never attempted to make me aware of the risk of having a total of 85 per cent exposure to equity and property markets.'

Rose's financial adviser denied liability, stating that she had accepted and signed three separate financial needs analysis documents.

The Financial Industry Complaints Service panel ruled that the adviser's executive summary effectively conveyed to Rose a guarantee of performance to the extent that her investments would increase in value at a minimum of 6 per cent above inflation.

'The recommendations in the executive summary are so positive that the complainant or a reasonable person in her position would not find it necessary to go through the whole of the plan or place much weight on the disclaimers if they did.'

The panel ruled the financial adviser should pay $30,000 (plus interest): this was calculated as the amount Rose would have received had her money been invested using a more conservative strategy.

Source: Adapted from Alan Kohler, *Eureka Report Guide to Personal Investing*, MUP, 2011

Inappropriate advice: Risk and investment loss

A couple, Mr and Mrs A, sought advice about investing $285,000. The couple aimed to purchase a business within three years but wanted to invest the amount in a short-term investment in the meantime. Their goal was to have a short-term income supplement of $25,000 per year.

Their financial planner recommended several investments, including putting $135,000 into an aggressive unlisted property trust that had a projected annual return of 20 per cent, or $27,000 per year. Eighteen months later, the property trust funds were frozen. Mr and Mrs A received frequent notices assuring them the trust would soon recover. Ultimately, however, administrators were appointed, and Mr and Mrs A were informed that their investment would not be repaid.

Mr and Mrs A complained that the financial planner had provided them with inappropriate advice. The financial planner denied liability, arguing that the advice was provided more than six years earlier, so the complaint was made outside the required time. The planner also submitted that, in any event, the advice was appropriate because Mr and Mrs A had previously held growth assets and had a relatively aggressive risk profile.

The Credit and Investments Ombudsman (CIO) decided the complaint was made within the permitted time because it was made within six years of Mr and Mrs A first becoming aware of their loss. Further, the CIO considered that a projected return of $27,000 per year would reasonably be seen as very aggressive for a short-term investment. The CIO concluded that the investment was **far riskier** than was required to achieve the investors' goals. Mr and Mrs A received compensation of $135,000 plus interest.

Source: Credit and Investments Ombudsman, 2018

The investment term and your time horizon

Your investment time horizon is how long you plan (or need) to invest your money, and it's a vital first step in investing. Knowing your goals will help define your time horizon. It will also help decide which asset classes are most suitable. For example, if you are investing for the short term, you might look at cash and fixed-interest asset classes, while a long-term outlook might be more suited to investing in Australian and international shares and property.

Age is important here. If you are young, and if your goal is to save for a comfortable retirement, then higher-risk, higher-return investments may be more suitable. But if your time horizon is much shorter – if, for example, you are approaching retirement, or if you are saving for a short-term goal like a car or perhaps a house deposit – then lower-risk, lower-return investments would make more sense. For those investments, your principal is better protected, and the timing of when you sell is less critical.

If, as an investor, you can master these concepts – risk, return and time – then the world will be yours.

Diversification

'Diversification' simply means not putting all your eggs in one basket. It means spreading your money out across multiple investments and types of investment, to reduce the risk of one of them blowing up. Diversifying across and within asset classes and geographic locations is the best insurance against all kinds of risk: country risk, sector risk and losses in single investments. After years of reporting on financial markets and personal finance, I'm still dismayed every time an exotic investment scheme collapses and investors lose their entire life savings. The investors shouldn't have put all their money in one spot, and a speculative one at that, and most of all advisers shouldn't have advised them to do it.

However, while diversification can lower risk, excessive diversification will guarantee an average performance. This is partly because high transaction costs and admin costs will erode your returns for no additional benefit, but also simply because if you end up with a bit of everything you'll also get the average of everything. You don't need hundreds of investments: 10 or 20 will usually do.

Liquidity

An investment is liquid if you can sell out quickly without bearing a significant exit cost; it's illiquid if you can't. And liquidity costs money – that is, the returns of illiquid investments tend to be higher than those of liquid ones, but not always. A managed fund, for example, can only be ready for investors to call on their money at short notice if it maintains significant cash reserves, or some other form of highly liquid assets. Being ready for quick withdrawals prevents the fund from pursuing potentially higher-earning investments, such as in private equity and infrastructure.

Australia's Future Fund has achieved consistently high returns, in part because it has less of a requirement for liquidity. The Future Fund's main job is to fund public sector superannuation. The Fund's cash requirements are predictable, and not immediate. This allows the Fund to invest in illiquid investments, such as ones that tie up money for five to ten years, or even longer. Such lumpy investments often perform well over the long term.

Other high-performing investments, too, have achieved high returns by accepting low liquidity: by being prepared to invest in lumpy assets over a long time horizon.

Collectively, I think Australian investors have too much liquidity. Like excessive diversification, excessive liquidity can erode your investment returns. Having your money 'at call' entails a cost. Ask yourself: do you need liquidity? If you don't need your money immediately, think about having some of your money in higher-returning illiquid investments.

For example, if you are twenty-five, you probably don't need any cash as part of your investment strategy – at all. The ideal investment for your super might involve zero cash and a very long timeline.

Taxation

Tax should never be your prime consideration in allocating assets or selecting an investment. Maximising investment returns is more important than minimising tax. Nevertheless, the impact of income tax on returns can be dramatic, especially for people on the top marginal tax rate, so it's absolutely essential to take into account when making investment decisions. It just shouldn't be the main thing.

When considering an investment or talking to a financial adviser, always ask about the impact of a particular investment option or decision on how much tax you will pay, given your income level and other circumstances. This especially applies when there's a choice between taking profits as capital gains or income. It's also worth noting that the ATO regulates super funds.

Inflation

'Inflation' refers to the general increase in the level of prices, particularly the prices of everyday goods and services such as food, clothing, travel and living costs. In recent years, inflation has been exceptionally low – and so, accordingly, have bond returns. There are several causes of the low inflation, including a 'digital productivity shock' (caused by matchers and disrupters such as Uber and Airbnb), environmentalism and 'green' values (which encourage lower consumption and greater reuse), and the exporting of goods-price deflation from China.

The oil shocks of the 1970s produced a once-in-a-generation spike in prices, and interest rates. There were actually two shocks – 1973, after the Yom Kippur War, and 1979, after the Iranian Revolution – and in those two jumps the price of oil went from $3 a barrel to $35, provoking a global economic crisis. The inflation had unexpected and wide-ranging effects on how companies were run, how they reported their performance, and how they sought investment. Asset values changed massively year on year, for example; how were companies to account for this? The whole system of capitalism was under incredible pressure.

For investors, inflation is worse than taxation as an eroder of returns. It can be devastating. Inflation of 3 per cent, for example, means that a 5 per cent return on a term deposit is really only a 2 per cent return. That's very likely not enough for you to achieve your investing goals.

6

Determining Your Strategy

THE MOST IMPORTANT FACTOR IN DECIDING what to do with your money and how to invest it is your stage of life. This is not the same as your age. Some people have kids and buy a house at age twenty (not many these days, admittedly), while others wait another ten or even twenty years. And the ages at which people retire vary wildly.

Each stage of life requires a different financial strategy, usually out of necessity. If you have a mortgage, then paying that off may be the only investment you can afford apart from compulsory super. And if you're retired, you probably need to invest for income, not long-term growth, because every dollar counts.

In this chapter I look into the particular issues and challenges for each stage of life, but these things are not necessarily exclusive. For example, just because you're not young doesn't mean compound interest and dollar-cost averaging have no relevance for you – we're all living a long time now! And just because you're not old doesn't mean income investing has no relevance. I recommend you read this whole chapter, regardless of your age and circumstances.

Young investors

Priorities for young investors

- Make the most of starting early by using dollar-cost averaging.
- Get your superannuation off to a good start.

Starting young is a beautiful thing – you've got lots of time, which means you can harness the power of compound interest, which Albert Einstein reportedly called the most powerful force in the universe. He meant that, given time, it can make you rich, but time is the main thing that's needed. The other good thing about starting young is that you are truly a long-term investor – you don't have to worry about all the inevitable ups and downs of markets that will happen along the way.

Dollar-cost averaging (DCA) is a good way to take advantage of those ups and downs. DCA is an investment strategy that involves investing a fixed dollar amount at regular intervals over time into something that goes up and down in price. That simply means that when the price is low, you buy more of it, and when it's high, you buy less. That's the exact opposite of what most people do when they're investing: when prices are flying and markets are euphoric, everyone tends to pile in and buy more; when the crash happens and everyone is suddenly in despair, everyone sells. When applied to share investing, for example, it means that when share prices are low, the fixed investment amount (say, $1000) buys a relatively large number of shares; and when prices are high, the same amount buys a smaller number of shares. So you're actually making the volatility work for you, instead of against you.

The simplest way to do it in practical terms would be to set up a direct debit into an ETF (exchange-traded fund) provider, or a super fund that uses units that go up and down in price (that is, they don't just put the cash into a pooled fund). Alternatively, you could just do it yourself, by setting up an account with an online broker like CommSec or Bell Direct and once a month investing the same amount into a listed investment company such as the Australian Foundation Investment Company (AFIC) or Argo Investments, or better still one of the riskier, higher return ones, like WAM Capital or Thorney Opportunities (since you're a long-term investor). You can find a list of them on the Australian Stock Exchange (ASX) website.

The reason DCA is a good idea is that the main killer of investment returns is making mistakes and losing money, usually by buying high and selling low. DCA helps you do the opposite – buy low and, although you don't sell when the price is high, at least you buy less.

That sort of approach has helped Warren Buffett make a compound return of 25 per cent over fifty years and, for a while, to become the world's richest person. To use our example above, if you put $100 away for fifty years at a compound annual growth rate of 25 per cent, you end up with . . . $7 million – and that's without doing any saving on top of that first $100! Save $100 a month at 25 per cent compound interest and you'll end up with $1 billion. Not that 25 per cent per annum is easy to come by, but most good fund managers can manage 15 per cent, especially with DCA, and that compound rate of return over 50 years, saving $100 a month, produces a final sum of $13.8 million.

Warren Buffett was worth $85 billion at the age of eighty-seven – he started young (twenty-one) and made 25 per cent a year compound over 66 years. You only need to start with $7000 at twenty-one to make $85 billion in sixty-six years if your compound interest is 25 per cent. (Come to think of it, I guess that means Buffett made some mistakes, and lost some money, because I think he started with more than $7000.)

There are a few reasons why DCA is a good idea:

- By reducing downside risk, it takes some of the gambling out of investing.
- It makes the investment amount more transparent, so too the extent of gains and losses.
- Regularity is a good habit.
- You can scale the investment to suit your personal circumstances, including your income and your goals.

Starting out with super

Superannuation is just saving with a tax break. The tax break is that money paid into super is only taxed at 15 per cent and earnings from super are taxed at 15 per cent as well. There are a few other complications, especially at the end, but they're the main ones. To get the tax break the money has to be locked up till you retire and it has to be in a qualifying fund, which can either be a big super fund, with lots of people's money in a pool, or a self-managed fund for just you and your family.

Self-managed funds are expensive to run, so there's not much use doing that while you're young – there's probably not enough money in the fund to make it worthwhile. So for most young investors, it's all about choosing a super fund or having it chosen for you.

My advice: choose it yourself. Don't let someone else choose it for you, even if they seem to have your interests at heart. Ignore all the marketing tosh and focus on the return, and a bit of googling will tell you which funds have the best returns. As discussed above, what you're trying to get – the only thing you're trying to get – is the greatest effect of compound interest over the long term, and while it's true, as they say in the advertising, that past returns are not a reliable guide to future returns, it's all you've got to go on. A super fund that has a good record of past returns is more likely to do well in future.

Apart from that, make sure you have only one fund and take it with you when you change jobs – don't let them start a new super account for you, no matter how hard they try.

And above all, remember this: even though the super deduction of 9.5 per cent of your salary is mandated by law, it's not a tax. *It's your money* (now there's a good title for a book!), and for most young people saving that percentage of your salary is plenty. Obviously if you've got a good job and can afford to save more, go ahead, but for most people anything left over should go into the mortgage – or perhaps a holiday. Life's tough!

The point is that super is you saving almost 10 per cent of your salary for retirement. You can take control of it. That doesn't mean investing it yourself, unless you really want to, but it can and should mean choosing who invests it for you, having checked up on how good they are and how much they charge. Keep thinking 'compound interest' – that is, high returns and low fees.

Investing in your thirties

Priorities for thirty-somethings

- Grow your after-tax income and (a big issue at this stage) reduce debt.
- Maintain a cash buffer for emergencies.
- Maintain adequate (but not excessive) life insurance and, possibly, income-protection insurance.
- Invest for the long term.
- Adopting a relatively aggressive investment approach, seeking higher-risk, higher-return investments.

For many people, this is a big stage in life. You're now more independent. You might be carrying credit card debts or other debts. You might be bearing the costs of your education, such as student loans. You might be struggling to pay rent, let alone enter the property market. And you might be planning to have children, or you might already have them. This is a time of juggling and of growing responsibilities.

It might sound obvious, but in your thirties the best way to build wealth is to put your head down and work hard. Better still, do it in your own business if you can, especially a business that can be sold (a lot can't because they're just you). A lot of people are starting to realise that, which is why creating a start-up – becoming an entrepreneur – is one of the fastest-growing career options these days and most universities have courses in entrepreneurship. Co-working hubs around the country are full of enterprising young optimists with a great idea trying to turn it into a business.

Not everyone can do that, of course. For most, it's all about salary growth, or doing some creative work that allows you to accumulate intellectual property that you can monetise, or just plain property (that is, a real estate investment). When your income rises, put as much as possible of the extra into your investments, not consumption.

But remember that debt is a kind of investment too, and paying off debt is usually a terrific way to invest, especially if it's a credit card or personal loan with high interest.

Paying off expensive debt is equivalent to earning a guaranteed high return (and one that is tax-free). If, for example, you make additional repayments on your 4 per cent home loan instead of paying down your 9 per cent car loan, then you are giving away the difference to people who probably don't deserve it. You should always pay off the most urgent and expensive debts first. Once these are cleared, you can focus on reducing less costly debt, such as the home mortgage.

Depending on your circumstances, some tax-effective strategies can include salary sacrificing into super, or using a family trust to direct income to a low-earning spouse. Even small amounts added to your super at this stage can make a big difference to your retirement nest egg. If you have a mortgage, a redraw facility can be a tax-effective place to put your cash buffer.

At the time of writing, an average super fund achieves around 7 per cent per annum. Some do much better than this; the difference between a good and a bad fund is very significant over the long term, as I've already noted. This is just one more reason why you have to take an active interest in the performance of your superannuation. I say it again: even though super is compulsory, it's your money, and you need to make deliberate decisions about it. Those decisions, and the best super strategies, vary at different stages of life.

If you are a youngish adult and contributing to superannuation, it makes sense to employ a more aggressive investment strategy, even if you are careful and conservative by nature. You have more time to ride out the inevitable volatility in investment markets, so investing in asset classes such as shares and property may enable you to grow your savings more aggressively, while maintaining peace of mind.

One way to earn tax-effective returns is via direct share investment and equity trusts, which can pay franked dividends. With franked dividends, a yield of 7 per cent is effectively equivalent to a 10 per cent return from a bond (ignoring risks). Property trusts also pay a high proportion of their annual unit-holder return as tax-exempt or tax-deferred income. Superannuation is the most tax-effective investment of all.

Don't let your personality type drive your approach to investing – within reason. Even if you are conservative by nature, you need to take some risks, especially early in life. But you also need to be able to sleep at night. Real estate markets are not subject to the same radical moves as the stock market. And property can be a high-performing long-term investment. Property investing, therefore, may be better for anxious investors. Property has another advantage, too: you can borrow against it, unlike shares. The ability to achieve leverage with property means total returns from real estate investing can outperform shares over the long run.

Investing in your mid-career years

Priorities for mid-career investors

- Take stock of where you are relative to where you'd like to be.
- Now is often a good time to balance your super towards higher growth and less liquid investments.
- Beware of self-managed super.
- Reinvest your tax refunds if you can.

If you're in your forties or fifties, it's half-time in the game of retirement saving – time to take stock. By taking stock – and to extend the metaphor – I mean, are you ahead or behind? Do you have to play harder in the third quarter and do some catching up, or are you coasting? If the latter: well done, you can probably skip this bit.

Most people, however, are probably at least a little behind where they'd like to be. That's because a lot of Australia's super funds, actually most of them, don't make a very good return.

For example, if you'd been saving an average of $800 a month for twenty years and getting the average balanced super fund return of 5.9 per cent per annum, your account would have around $365,000 in it at age forty-five. You'd probably look at that and think: 'Crikey! I'm going to fall short!' (At least you would if you'd read this book and knew how the super system works.)

And you'd be right. If you kept going on that return for another twenty years, you'd end up with $1.6 million, which is exactly the amount the government has chosen as the cut-off for tax-free lump sums. In fact, it's roughly enough to make sure you won't qualify for the old-age pension.

Here are my steps for taking action if you're behind at half-time:

1. DON'T PANIC. You've still got twenty years left. Which is a long time – time enough to make compound interest work its magic for you. What I mean is: you don't need to roll the dice and risk your family's wealth by punting the lot on a spec miner.

2. Have a good look at your super fund. Perhaps talk to them about high-growth options and what they've been returning. Think about switching options within your existing fund.

3. If all the returns of your fund over the past twenty years are not flash, including high-growth options, do some shopping around, and move to a fund with a ten-year return history of at least 10 per cent. The Hostplus Balanced option, for example, has earned 12.5 per cent per annum for ten years. If you moved your $365,000 to a fund that earns 12.5 per cent per annum for the next twenty years, and kept saving $800 a month, you would end up with $4.5 million, not the $1.6 million you would get with a return of 5.9 per cent. (Of course, you can't guarantee you'll get 12.5 per cent return, only make it more likely).

4. Should you get the money out of the big super fund and start your own – a self-managed super fund (SMSF)? Maybe. You've almost got enough that the administration costs (auditing and filing tax returns) won't be any more in percentage terms than the big super fund. But be careful: most people with SMSFs employ an expensive adviser charging 1 to 1.5 per cent

on top of the fund managers' fees. You could be forking out $5000 a year for something that in a big super fund effectively costs nothing, which is asset allocation guidance. And doing it yourself could be like rewiring the house on your own instead of hiring an electrician – you could get a nasty shock.

5. If you are already making the maximum concessionary contributions to super, and you have equity in your house, consider buying an investment property (if you haven't already done so, of course). Although given the softness in the housing market at the moment, especially in Melbourne and Sydney, there's no hurry. If you rent, and have some spare cash, consider buying an investment property for the negative gearing. The combination of negative gearing and the capital gains tax discount, plus the potential for relatively high gearing, make residential property investments about as tax-friendly as super.

In general, now is the time to make some decisions about your retirement, that is: how much will you need to live on. I know it's hard to work that out twenty years ahead of time, but it's important. That decision will set the bar for what you have to achieve over the next two decades. As a conservative rule of thumb, you'll need a capital sum about fifteen times what you want in income, after tax, so $5000 a month cash would require capital of $1 million.

But don't forget that you could qualify for a part-pension as well. The means test rules can be found on the Department of Human Services website under 'Age Pension' eligibility.

The Canadian scholar and finance writer Moshe Milevsky has argued that the nature of your work should determine how you invest in your peak earning years. According to Milevsky, people with relatively certain income – public servants, academics and so on – should take more risks with their investments. They should even consider borrowing to increase their exposure to shares and growth assets. But people with less certain prospects – investment bankers, entrepreneurs, equity-owning executives – should have a smaller proportion (no more than 60 per cent) of their money in shares.

✓ **Tip:** Historically, the correlation between the performance of growth assets – such as international and Australian shares – and defensive assets – such as fixed interest – has been low. When one asset class is up, the other is down, or up to a lesser extent. Fixed-interest investments can provide investors with a natural balance to their growth assets.

✓ **Tip:** Reinvest your tax refunds if possible. The power of compounding means that even small additional payments over time can make a big difference by reducing the amount of interest you are paying on your debt or increasing the interest you are earning on your investments.

Investing towards the end of your working life

Priorities towards the end of your working life
- Reduce risk and exposure to volatility, because you don't want to be trying to access your cash from the stock market when it is in the middle of a correction.
- Reduce any remaining debts.
- Develop an explicit plan for retirement that includes a tax-effective structure.
- Revisit your life insurance.
- Invest for the long term (still), but rebalance towards less aggressive investments, more focused on capital preservation, with incrementally more liquidity.
- Focus your financial resources on boosting your retirement savings, preferably as superannuation.

While superannuation may be a long-term investment for many people, if you are approaching retirement age you may want to focus on preserving your capital and employ a capital-protection strategy that invests in defensive assets such as fixed interest and cash.

It's getting a bit late now to do much about it, but if you haven't already worked out how much you will need in retirement, it's definitely time to do so. This question has attracted much recent attention and is hotly debated. As discussed in the previous section, a reasonable goal – and a sensible rule of thumb – is to build up capital equivalent to fifteen times your desired annual retirement income. So, if your goal is an annual net income of $60,000, you will need around $1 million.

Many retirees worry that they will outlive their investments. This is a valid concern given the size of our super and the length of our lives. One way to manage this risk is to stay in the workforce longer, perhaps part-time. This can be great for mental health and social engagement, and you can continue to contribute to super up to age seventy-five while you are still working. These are the sorts of questions you need to work through with your financial adviser in preparing your retirement plan.

Investing during retirement

Priorities for retirees

- Implement your retirement plan.
- Keep some of your wealth as liquid assets such as term deposits.
- Structure your affairs to optimise eligibility for post-retirement entitlements.
- Review your insurance, including health cover.
- Invest for the medium and long term.
- Keep your nest egg as superannuation for as long as you can.

A good financial planner should be able to help you minimise, or even eliminate, tax at this stage of life. The basic rule at the moment (and with the way successive governments have been tinkering with these rules, it could change at any time) is that if you're over sixty, the first $1.6 million is tax-free, as long as you satisfy the conditions of release (that is, you retire). There was no limit between July 2007 and July 2017, and before 2007 it was strictly limited. This means that in many ways sixty is the new sixty-five (that used to be the key retirement age), but sixty-five is still an important age as well. That's when you can access your super without retiring.

I think a key decision at retirement is: how much do you want to leave the kids when you die? If you don't have any kids, that's a pretty easy decision. And if your super balance and other assets are such that you need to eat into them through your retirement, that's also an easy decision. But for many people, there's a balance to be struck between living well in retirement and leaving some kind of inheritance. Then again, a lot of people (like me) decide to do some "early inheritance" – after all, the kids need it now, and I plan to live a long time.

I haven't retired yet, but I'd like to die with the same amount of money that I retire with – that is, no need to grow the capital: I just want to live off it. My kids have decent jobs and are financially okay, so I want to invest for income in retirement, not growth, but I'd like to try to preserve the capital for my grandchildren. Having said that, I might live a long time (my mum has just turned 90 and my dad died at 88), so maybe some growth would be a good idea.

You should hold some of your assets in a liquid form – such as term deposits with staggered maturities. You need enough cash at call to cover your lump-sum needs on retirement and on-going spending requirements for eighteen months to two years in advance.

I see many cases where someone reaches retirement and with-draws all the money from their super fund. Withdrawing money from super upon retirement can start a costly yet pointless cycle, especially if the super fund has products specifically aimed at people in retirement, as most super funds do. Another adviser invests it, taking 1 per cent or more plus transaction costs and tax; prepares a $3000 financial plan (not an atypical cost); then reinvests the money pretty much back where it was. It's a cycle of theft, and is largely keeping the financial advice industry going, pointlessly.

✓ **Tip:** Consolidate your super into one place if you haven't already.

The superannuation industry bears some of the blame here. Super funds have not been good at convincing people to leave some or all of their money in such funds after retirement, partly because they think they are in the saving business rather than the retirement income business.

Whenever I get the chance, I tell super fund managers and trustees that they have got their business wrong: they market their ability to invest rather than their ability to provide a comfortable retirement. As a result, they have allowed a mentality to develop in which the moment of retirement is seen as the end of the relationship with the super fund, and is a signal to shift money out of the fund and into a bank account – or perhaps to the bank account of a cruise operator, or some other place. Super funds should be encouraging people to leave their money in super for longer.

The longer you leave your money invested in super, the longer compound interest has to weave its magic and create a substantial nest egg for your retirement, and the less money the government needs to spend on the age pension and other welfare benefits in the future.

An investor could hold an identical portfolio of shares, property, bonds and other investments inside a super fund or outside one. Investments held inside super are subject to the same market fluctuations as those held outside super, as well as the same gross annual returns, but tax concessions, lower fees (with industry funds, not retail ones) and the length of time the investments are left to grow inside super generally produce a better return on your money.

Investment earnings inside your super fund are taxed at a maximum rate of 15 per cent. If your fund owns Australian shares with franked dividends, then your fund will pay less than 15 per cent tax. This is less than half the tax most individuals would pay on the same investments if they held them outside super. The vast majority of working Australians pay tax at a marginal rate of between 31.5 per cent and 46.5 per cent, including the Medicare levy.

Capital gains on the sale of assets within super also receive favourable tax treatment. If the asset has been held for more than twelve months, the fund only pays tax on two-thirds of the capital gain, at a rate of 15 per cent. This is an effective tax rate on capital gains of 10 per cent (two-thirds of 15 per cent). If you held the same investments outside super for twelve months, you would pay tax at your marginal rate on half the capital gain, an effective tax rate of 15 per cent for low-income earners but up to 23.25 per cent for investors on the top marginal rate.

✓ **Tip:** While non-preserved funds can be accessed before retirement, investing them back into your superannuation fund makes sense because you could pay much more tax on these funds if you invest them outside of super.

Your pension entitlements are important. You should claim any pension you are entitled to: even a small part-pension will make you eligible for a range of discounts and benefits. For obvious reasons, you should make sure you have adequate health insurance cover.

If you only have a relatively short investment horizon, you can't afford to take big risks. You need to focus on capital protection and accept lower returns. Usually, though, capital protection in retirement is important but not the only goal; there is a good argument for leaving at least part of your portfolio in assets such as shares and property that will grow in value.

My top ten tips for investing at all stages of life

1. Get good advice.
2. Stay in control.
3. Tend to your portfolio and your adviser relationships like a thoughtful gardener.
4. Diversify across asset classes – say, shares or property – as well as within asset classes.
5. But don't overdo diversification. For smaller investors, a common mistake with diversification is to diversify too much. It simply isn't true that the more things you invest in, the less risk you are taking. You don't need to have hundreds of investments: 10 or 20 will usually do.
6. Don't buy too much liquidity.
7. Copying a strategy that was successful for someone else in the past is no guarantee of success for you in the future.
8. Time in the market gives you the opportunity to take bigger, calculated risks in pursuit of higher returns.
9. One of the biggest mistakes investors can make is to confuse luck with skill.
10. If something seems too good to be true ...

7

Real Estate

I COULD WRITE A WHOLE BOOK ABOUT INVESTING IN real estate, but it's been done already (many times). For this book, let's just focus on whether to, and how to, invest in it.

First, let's remember a few fundamentals. People rent houses, not land, but only land goes up in value. Houses depreciate. To be a successful real estate investor you must understand that the house or apartment is the basis of your income, so maintaining it properly is the key to maximising yield, but capital growth only comes from the land.

Second, there are only two things that matter with a piece of land: how big it is, and where it is. Yes, 'location, location, location' is a cliché, but it's true: it's the thing you can't change and it determines the ultimate resale value. I've learnt this the hard way, with houses I've owned, including a house in Paddington that had rising damp, falling damp and every other kind of damp, and a house in Coogee that had great ocean views. There is much more to a location than a view, but a view helps.

The thing is, no one's making any more land – it has scarcity value. Even in a large and lightly populated country such as Australia, there is a scarcity of land where people want to live and work – in major towns and cities, and near the coast and other natural attractions. As our population increases, the scarcity value of land is likely to increase (although it is vulnerable to technologies that make transport faster and more efficient).

Investing in real estate is both complicated and appealingly simple. What I mean is that on the one hand property is a hard market to get your head around, but on the other a house is real – something you can physically walk around in – whereas a company share doesn't even exist on paper anymore, it's just ones and zeroes in a computer somewhere.

Why is the property market complicated? Well, for a start there's no single market. Every state, city, suburb, even street, is a market all its own. In fact, every house and apartment is different in its own way. Prices in Sydney might be going down while those in Hobart are going up. Each suburb within a city moves at a different pace. And then there are the differences between types of properties, within each geographic segment. There are markets for vacant land, new housing construction, new and old commercial property, existing houses, new and existing apartments, posh waterfront houses, and Californian bungalows in Randwick, and even property securities (which you can't walk around in). But perhaps the main reason property investing is complicated is that it's emotional. Houses are what we live in, and it's hard to separate the tug of domesticity from the act of investing. In fact, most people who own both a home and an investment property tend to invest near where they live. Nothing wrong with that – after all, you tend to know that area best of all – but it rather breaks the rule about diversification in investing.

One of the reasons property is popular as an investment, apart from the emotional reason mentioned above, is that the bank will generally lend more against real estate: borrow to buy shares and you'll be lucky to get 50 per cent of the value, but the typical loan-to-value ratio for property is 80 per cent. That means property investments tend to perform really well when prices are rising, but of course the debt means the falls are exaggerated as well.

The only other thing to mention upfront is that when you buy a place to live in, you're also investing, except there is a big difference between buying your own home versus buying an investment property. In my view, you should never buy a home as if you're buying an investment property, and vice versa. They are two entirely different things: a home is where you're going to live, and love, perhaps raise a family, whereas an investment is bought for the best return – the best rent and the best resale value. Whether you like it or you'd want to live in it has nothing to do with it. It's really just about emotion versus hard-nosed detachment. If there's one lesson I'd like to pass on about property investing it's this: if you love the place, don't do it – it's probably a mistake.

> **AUSTRALIANS LOVE REAL ESTATE, BUT ...**
> According to the Australian Bureau of Statistics, the total value of our 10 million homes is approaching $7 trillion, after passing the $6 trillion mark in June 2016. The housing market is, however, subject to cycles, and rates of home ownership also fluctuate.

Home ownership

For many decades, the proportion of Australians who owned (or were paying off) their own home remained remarkably stable, at around 70 per cent. But in recent years the proportion has fallen, especially among younger age groups. Research published in 2017 by the Grattan Institute and using census data found home ownership was declining among people aged under fifty-five, and even more rapidly for 25- to 34-year-olds. In 1986, 58 per cent of people in that age group owned their home. In 2017, however, the proportion was 45 per cent, and the drop has been especially sharp in the last decade.

It used to be a rule of thumb that your initial loan repayments should not be more than 30 per cent of your pre-tax income. In the property boom, however, many people apparently threw caution to the wind, committing to a much higher percentage. That exposed people to all sorts of risks, especially in a softening market.

Buying your own home can be a pathway to property investment, as you can borrow against your equity. Since the 1980s, rising property prices have enabled many investors to leverage the value in their own home, using the capital gain to invest in other property. As a result, more investors than ever before are involved in the property sector.

This has had several effects, including creating lots of 'mini-moguls' in the property sector, and perhaps making it even more difficult for younger people to own property. In a falling market, the mini-moguls face all sorts of risks, and the people who've been mostly on the sidelines during the boom – well, they've got all sorts of opportunities.

Bricks and mortar

My wife, Deb, prefers investing in property and hates it when I invest in companies, and many people are the same. They like the fact that you can actually walk around in and touch what you've bought. (In the days of share certificates, investing in companies was a much more tangible experience than it is today – now you don't even get a piece of paper.) The good long-term investment performance of property is also difficult to ignore. It is also easier to borrow against property compared with other investments, and banks will lend you more against property (although that's not why Deb likes it).

The 'bricks and mortar' character of property does have a downside. Property is a lumpy, illiquid asset: you can't sell it off room by room when you need cash. This aspect of property tends to encourage home owners and investors to hold on to real estate for longer.

> **PROPERTY AND SHARE INVESTMENT PERFORMANCE**
> According to the 2018 Russell Investments/ASX Long Term Investing Report:
> - Australian shares returned 4 per cent in the ten years to December 2017.
> - Australian residential property returned 8 per cent over the same period.
> - Global shares (hedged) returned 7.2 per cent over the period.
> - Australian listed property returned just 1.8 per cent.
> - Over twenty years, the relative returns of Australian shares and property were closer – 8.8 per cent and 10.2 per cent respectively – but houses still out-performed shares.
> - Different time periods can demonstrate the cyclical nature of any asset class, even property. For example, during the 1990s, the best-performing asset class in the ten-year periods up to 1991, 1992, 1993, 1994, 1998, 1999, 2000 and 2001 was international shares.

Favourable tax treatment and government subsidies are not the only reasons why buying your own home can be a sound investment. Paying off or into the mortgage is an important discipline. It is a form of forced saving, and an effective way to start building wealth. The majority of home buyers elect to pay more than their minimum monthly mortgage repayment to reduce debt and build equity. You can use this additional equity as a cash buffer to draw on for emergencies, but the less you dip into it the better.

Once you have sufficient equity in your home – 50 per cent is a good rule of thumb – you can use this to borrow money to kickstart an investment portfolio. A home equity loan is generally cheaper then alternative forms of finance such as margin loans.

Australia's obsession with real estate has a dark side. Do you remember Henry Kaye's 'get rich quick' style of property seminars and schemes? In the 1990s and 2000s, charismatic spruikers used high-pressure techniques to rush investors into decisions – and it's still going on to some extent. The spruikers pitched their seminars as 'educational' events rather than financial advice; this was just an attempt to avoid regulatory rules around the provision of financial advice. They were promoting 'strategy', they claimed, rather than 'advice'. They were 'educating' rather than 'selling'.

High-octane property investment scams were rampant in the property sector. The provision of property investment 'advice' and 'wealth-creation' seminars was rife with:

- false representations that property investments are risk-free or low risk
- the old problem of undisclosed commissions and other charging arrangements
- the equally old problem of undisclosed relationships between promoters and property developers
- difficulties in getting refunds of money spent on seminars and courses
- difficulties in suing 'fly by night' spruikers.

Today, the provision of property advice is still one of the least regulated areas of the Australian financial services industry and there are still plenty of 'get rich quick' scammers trying to take advantage of the high sales commissions offered by developers looking to quickly unload blocks of apartments. Regulation of property in general is uneven, and historically consumer protection has been weak. Rules vary from state to state on important matters such as 'dummy bidding' and the protection of owners in multi-unit developments. There is significant confusion and duplication in the role of regulators such as ASIC, the ACCC and state-based consumer affairs agencies.

REIA NATIONAL PRINCIPLES OF CONDUCT

The Real Estate Institute of Australia's 'Principles of Conduct' emphasise the duty to act in clients' interests. They aim to promote and encourage a high standard of ethical practice by REI members and their employees in all dealings with clients, consumers, real estate professionals, regulators and the general public.

REI members shall:

1. hold the required professional qualifications, insurances and indemnities necessary to operate within their state or territory.
2. have a reasonable knowledge and understanding and act in accordance with the relevant laws governing the real estate profession, including codes of conduct, these principles and the rules of professional associations.
3. maintain and improve their knowledge, skills and qualifications over the course of their career.
4. act in the best interests of their client and in accordance with their instructions except where it would be unreasonable or improper to do so.
5. act ethically, fairly and honestly when dealing with all parties and not allow any person to believe that they are acting for any party other than their client.

6. treat fellow real estate agents with respect and profes-
    sional courtesy. REI members shall disclose their role to
    all other agents involved in a property transaction.

7. not use or disclose any confidential information obtained
    while acting on behalf of their client or dealing with a
    customer, except for information that members are
    required by law to disclose.

8. endeavour to prevent or resolve disputes with a view
    to minimising the number of complaints made against
    the real estate agent. REI members will inform all com-
    plainants of the alternate avenues of complaint open
    to them.

9. disseminate relevant information received from, or
    required by, the REIA or REI where this will assist the
    ongoing development of the profession. REI members
    shall actively seek to continually improve the status and
    general operation of the real estate profession for the
    benefit of clients and customers.

Good legal advice is essential if you plan to navigate the property sector. Different laws and protections apply to property investment compared to other forms of investment. For the purposes of
some key laws relating to investment, real estate is not regarded as
a financial product. The issues are similar but the protections are
often weaker for property.

A genuinely independent property adviser will charge you a
fee. When it comes to getting good property advice, a key principle is: there is no such thing as free advice. This applies to all
investments.

Real estate can provide an 'inflation hedge' – that is, an investment whose value is expected to rise in times of inflation.

Warren Buffett recommends a 'buy and hold' strategy for shares. I've heard other people say the same about real estate – that you should never sell unless you absolutely have to.

PARENTS LENDING TO THEIR CHILDREN
FOR PROPERTY INVESTMENT

In 2018 the *AFR* reported that the 'Bank of Mum and Dad' had become one of the biggest banks in the country. In fact, it was Australia's tenth largest lender, 'bigger than ME Bank, AMP Bank and the local operations of global banking giants like Citigroup and HSBC Australia.' This growth is not without risk. Lending to your children can be cheaper (if you have money to lend), but this is partly an illusion, as you might bear the cost of a possible default. And mixing family and finance can be a minefield both legally and emotionally. How to protect yourself and any offspring you might have? Seek advice from your financial planner, your financial institution, industry sources and comparison sites – and people who know you well as a person, and whom you can trust.

✓ **Tip:** Real estate is a good place for anxious investors. Real estate markets move less than stock markets, and they move more slowly.

✓ **Tip:** Real estate can be a good alternative to shares, managed funds and super – because you can borrow against it, and use the leverage to increase your returns.

Property investment risks and pitfalls

There are many risks and pitfalls with property investment, including:

- problems in finding the right property at the right price
- problems in settlement
- problems with agents and tenants
- cyclical problems: if interest rates rise, for example, repayments can become difficult
- unmet expectations – the investment may not make the return you desire, or the returns you need in order to optimise your use of gearing
- unexpected costs, such as major maintenance and damage costs
- changes in the rules, such as for negative gearing and capital gains tax.

√ **Tip:** Always read the fine print. It is where wicked surprises sometimes lurk, and it is often the difference between a good and a bad investment.

√ **Tip:** Beware complex investment structures.

PROS AND CONS OF OPENING YOUR HOME
TO PAYING GUESTS

In this new era of digital intermediaries and 'matching markets', many people have opened parts of their own home (as well as whole properties they own) to paying guests via Airbnb and similar start-ups and portals. This can provide a supplementary income, but it is not without costs and risks. Some body corporates and local councils place restrictions on the extent to which homes can be used for this purpose. Some Airbnb landlords are finding that the effort involved – such as regularly cleaning and administering short-stay properties – can be onerous. And then there is the stress and the spectacle caused by scammers and gatecrashers who use short-stay rentals as a way to arrange party venues, and to get themselves on the evening news and into the magistrate's court. More than one Airbnb host has switched back to longer-term leasing through the conventional rental market.

Residential property investment strategy

Buying property, like buying shares, is not a place for sentiment and emotion. Also like shares, there is no such thing as 'good' or 'bad' real estate, or a 'good' or 'bad' location (or not many anyway) – provided the price is right. From the point of view of the direct property investor, a one-bedroom unit in a popular location is not necessarily better than one next to the airport. The latter property might have a higher rental yield and more room for capital growth. In property, as in shares, you get what you pay for.

When choosing a property, you need to do your research. The decision to buy should be based on the fundamentals, not on aesthetics or personal preferences. Look for the towns and suburbs that are expected to grow the fastest over the next three to five years and beyond. This should provide capital growth and could allow regular rent increases. Vacancy rates can give you an idea of the likely demand for rental property in a particular area. Not all suburbs are the same: vacancy rates in the same city can range from close to zero to more than 12 per cent, depending on where we are in the economic cycle. (Vacancy rates can usually be found on websites like domain.com.au.)

It is a good idea to inspect the property and explore the local area before you purchase. This way, you can make sure you know what you are buying. After all, if everything goes pear-shaped, you might end up living there!

✓ **Tip:** Houses tend to have better capital appreciation, while apartments often have better rental yields.

✓ **Tip:** The real estate industry is full of people who claim they can beat the market. They can't.

QUEST SERVICED APARTMENTS

Quest is among the most well-known brands in Australia's serviced apartment market. As Simon Johanson reported in *The Sydney Morning Herald* in 2018, some investors in Quest apartments have hit problems due to the fine print of long-term lease agreements. Terms in those agreements have allowed property managers to make decisions about capital investment, and to revalue properties in ways that have reduced investment returns; and they have locked people in for long periods.

The experience of David Lawrance, former ACT Commissioner of Tourism, is a case in point. In the early 2000s, David bought a Quest apartment for $215,000 on Punt Road, Windsor, in Melbourne, having been advised to do this by his financial planner.

David and his wife hoped to rely on the investment to supplement their income. The investment promised steady returns with annual 4 per cent increases over the life of a four-by-five year (i.e. twenty-year) lease agreement. The apartment returned about $19,000 per year in rent.

The problems began when much of the rental return was offset by urgent repairs. David's family was sent a notice requiring more than $40,000 in repairs to the property. Quest's franchisee also reset the rental rate to 20 per cent below the previous period, after an independent valuation reduced the property's value. And because the lease was commercial rather than residential, its terms were set for the full 20 years.

When David and his family decided to sell the property, they received $280,000. 'Over a fifteen-year period,' Simon Johanson wrote, 'it gained $65,000 in value, well below Melbourne's average capital growth rate. Unencumbered by a commercial lease to Quest, the property would have fetched around $400,000 on the open market.'

Direct property investment: Costs and management

Property investing is heavy with transaction costs such as stamp duty, lender's mortgage insurance, conveyancing and building inspections. It is often financed with an interest-only loan to conserve capital and boost cash flow, and frequently one with a redraw or offset facility. Additional equity held in this way can be used as a cash buffer to draw on in emergencies.

Direct property investments are either managed by you or through a real estate agent, who typically charges a 5 per cent annual management fee (or more). Some residential property investors try to cut costs by managing the property themselves. This is almost always a case of false economy. Using an agent saves you time and stress, and helps you avoid personal conflict with tenants.

For property purchases and sales, you need to watch management charges and investigate what costs you would incur if you needed to access your funds before the nominated termination date. Make a full inventory of all the costs associated with your property investment, particularly direct property investing. Government charges can add up, so make sure you know all the costs when considering property investment options.

Stamp duty is a big problem – and a big disincentive – in direct property investment. It is a state government tax and it is the largest initial cost of buying a property, apart from the initial deposit. Each state has a different stamp duty rate. State government land tax may also be payable on the unimproved value of land. You should check what rules apply in your state before making any property investment. Council rates and utilities, including water, electricity and gas, are also important day-to-day costs of investing in direct property.

Tax and property investment

The family home is fully exempt from capital gains tax (CGT). But note that this may not be the case if you use part of the home for conducting a business. You should seek advice on the tax treatment of stamp duty, legal costs, property improvements and loan establishment fees from your accountant. Some costs are not tax-deductible but can be added to the cost base of the property and taken into account for CGT purposes when the property is sold. Some costs can be written off over time.

Engaging an agent

The growth in the property market has caused a surge in demand for property advice. A key source of advice for buyers and investors is the buyer's agent, who operates under a normal real estate agent's licence, but explicitly on behalf of the buyer. Whichever type of agent you engage, there are pitfalls – and sometimes conflicting incentives. You need to be careful. Some possible questions to ask, to help manage these risks, are shown overleaf. If an agent can't answer these in a way that satisfies you, look elsewhere for help and advice.

Whose interests?

When it comes to selling a home, engaging a real estate agent is crucial. Hiring an agent is a lot like hiring a financial planner. We place a large slice of our wealth in the agent's hands, and we trust that he or she will act in our interests.

But will the agent actually do that? Steven Levitt and Stephen Dubner found that estate agents, like commission-earning financial planners, were not putting their clients' interests first. As they pointed out in *Freakonomics*, the estate agents' incentive is to get a sale in order to earn a commission. This means tempering sellers' expectations. Agents also shirk effort: putting in a few more hours to wring a better price for the seller often isn't worth it in terms of the increment to the agent's commission.

QUESTIONS TO ASK A REAL ESTATE ADVISER

- What will you do to understand my needs and ensure your advice is suitable for me?
- How do you make sure that you act in my interests and deliver value for money?
- What types of services do you provide? What types do you not provide? Do you have unrestricted access to the property market? What after-purchase services do you offer?
- How are you and your company compensated? Are you subject to any conflicts of interest?
- What experience do you have in advising purchasers on property acquisitions? How many years have you been in this sector? What experience do you have specifically with direct residential property?
- What formal qualifications do you and your colleagues hold? What ongoing professional education do you undertake?
- Are you and your company licensed?
- What data and research is your advice based on?
- What is your fee, and will you negotiate it?

Listed property investment vehicles

'Securitisation' is an awful word in several senses. In the case of property, it means bundling up a group of assets – various pieces or forms of commercial property – and issuing securities to investors via a managed trust or fund. Such funds give private investors a practical means to gain exposure to commercial property in Australia and overseas.

There are many different types of listed property vehicles. They each have their own risks, transaction costs and tax implications. The different options all vary with respect to legal rights, yields, lease duration, type of finance and levels of fees. This is not a place for novices.

Real estate investment trusts (REITs)

While Australians love the tangible nature of property investing, tangibility can also be a downside. That's because real estate is illiquid. Selling property is not the easiest or quickest thing to do, and transaction costs can be high for both sellers and buyers.

Hence the interest in an alternative way to invest in property: real estate investment trusts (REITs). These are professionally managed trusts that specialise in property. They invest in a wide range of commercial property types, giving investors access to the industrial, office, hotel, leisure and retail property sectors, both in Australia and overseas (A-REITs and global REITs).

According to the ASX, the advantages of buying and selling REITs include the following:

- You have easy and immediate access to the REIT of your choice as purchases and sales are done during normal ASX trading hours.
- There is flexibility to use 'limit orders' to buy and sell at prices you specify.
- Information on your investments is easily accessible in newspapers and websites.
- Transactions are settled in three days.
- If your transaction or holding is subject to fraud or insolvency of your licensed adviser, the National Guarantee Fund may cover your losses.
- REITs are subject to supervision through initial and ongoing ASX requirements.

Because REITs are listed on the stock market, units can be bought and sold in a matter of hours. However, they are also more volatile, and prices tend to fluctuate with market movements.

Property can be a difficult asset class in which to achieve diversification. REITs can come to the rescue here. By investing through a REIT, you can gain access to a range of property sub-types and sub-sectors.

REITs come in various legal structures and they vary in how they operate. Typically, they make quarterly or twice-yearly distributions of the rental income received from the underlying properties. There is also potential for capital growth. REITs can have tax benefits for some types of investors; ask your accountant about this.

Although REITs are still popular with some retirees and other investors, they are not necessarily low risk. Some funds have a high level of borrowings, which, as I've already noted, can magnify losses as well as gains.

REITs borrow up to around 30 to 40 per cent against the assets they own. This means that for every million dollars they hold, around $700,000 is investors' money, and $300,000 is debt. But most REITs charge investors a fee that corresponds to the whole value of the assets, including the part that is funded by the borrowings. The fees are fairly low, so investors are generally prepared to live with this arrangement.

On the stock exchange, REITs often trade at up to 1.2 times the value of their underlying net assets. This reflects the potential for growth in the value of the assets, and the ability of REIT managers to extract income from them.

Over the past 100 years or so, shares slightly outperformed real estate. But investors in real estate still often did better due to the effects of leverage, which magnified the returns from property.

Final thoughts on real estate

Here are two quotes about investing in real estate.

Real estate cannot be lost or stolen, nor can it be carried away. Purchased with common sense, paid for in full, and managed with reasonable care, it is about the safest investment in the world.

FRANKLIN D. ROOSEVELT

Ninety percent of all millionaires become so through owning real estate. More money has been made in real estate than in all industrial investments combined. The wise young man or wage earner of today invests his money in real estate.

ANDREW CARNEGIE

So which is it? The safest investment, or the best way to get rich?

It's neither, really, and it's both at the same time. Real estate can be very risky, and also very slow – it depends how much you borrow, what you buy and when you buy it. Buy an overpriced McMansion at the top of the market with borrowed money and you'll quickly go bust. But it's also true that a lot of very rich people have made their money from property, by buying well, at the right time.

My main problem with residential real estate as an investment is that it's hard to diversify prudently unless you have a lot of money, because you generally have to buy a whole house or apartment, whereas share investing can be done in very small lots.

These days, thanks to technology, there are a few ways to invest in fractions of properties, and it's an area that's growing in sophistication and maturity. We can only hope.

8

Shares

EVERYONE INVESTS IN SHARES, WHETHER THEY know it or not. That's because superannuation in Australia is compulsory and all super funds own shares on behalf of their members. Even if you think shares are a mug's game and you're all about real estate, sorry, but the chances are you own some shares too. Perhaps you are retired and a financial adviser helps you with your money – investing in shares. Or you might come into share ownership as a result of your work or an inheritance, or some other way. However you encounter shares, you need to know some fundamentals about them.

Shares are little slices of companies and should be approached that way, in my view, not as an 'asset class' or 'equities'. When you buy a share, or put money into super, you buy into a business. You become a part-owner, and you have a stake in the company's success. You also have important rights, including an entitlement to a share of any profits that are distributed (if it makes any) and (for ordinary shares) the right to vote at shareholder meetings.

The profit entitlement arrives in the form of a dividend. In Australia, dividends may be 'franked', which means they carry with them a pre-payment of any tax that has been paid by the company. Shareholders get a credit for that tax that's been paid, so, depending on your circumstances, this can make shares more tax-effective in your hands.

Companies usually pay dividends twice a year, in the form of an interim and final dividend, although some companies might forgo one or both of these payments, or they might pay additional special dividends. And of course, a lot of companies don't make any money, so they can't pay a dividend.

When directors announce a dividend, they provide three key dates: the day the shares will trade 'ex-dividend', the 'record date', and the 'date payable'. Shares are quoted on the ASX as ex-dividend four business days before the record date, when the company closes its register to determine which shareholders are eligible to receive the dividend. You must be the registered owner of the shares on the ex-dividend date if you want to receive the dividend.

Once the shares begin trading ex-dividend, the price generally falls in line with the amount of the dividend – because after that date, buyers are not entitled to the payment. To check whether a share is trading ex-dividend, see the share tables in the financial press or on the ASX website.

Public and private companies

Some major companies are 'private' and 'unlisted', which means they are owned by a small number of institutions and/or individuals – perhaps family members and relatives of the company's founders. Stakes in the ownership of the company are not traded on a public market. High-profile private companies in Australia include Visy, Queensland Sugar and the Grocon group.

'Listed' public companies, in contrast, have their shares traded on a stock exchange. They are almost always 'limited liability' companies (hence the Ltd after their names), which means the liability of shareholders is limited to what they have put in – they can't be asked to pay the debts as well if the company goes broke.

Investors can buy and sell their shares at prices set by other buyers and sellers in the open market. Listed companies must comply with listing rules and requirements. These usually relate to trading, reporting and how companies are structured. To list on the ASX, for example, companies must be a certain size and they must keep the market informed by reporting profits, losses and other financial information that could have a bearing on share prices.

Types of shares

Not all companies and shares are the same. In fact, they come in enormous variety: different industry sectors, different company sizes, different classes of shares, and different risk and return characteristics. Companies that have stable dividends and low share-price volatility are prized for their defensive characteristics, while speculative stocks offer potentially high growth (and high risk) with little or no income. An example of a popular stable dividend stock is the Commonwealth Bank, which has been steadily increasing its dividend ever since it was privatised in 1992. All stocks are volatile to some extent, but one of the least volatile is Transurban, because its toll roads are such stable businesses (it also pays a stable dividend as well). Perhaps the greatest Australian example of a growth stock is CSL, privatised in 1994 and delivering growth of 25 per cent per annum ever since – $1000 invested in CSL when it was listed, and left there to grow with dividends reinvested, would now be worth $400,000. Now that's a growth stock.

Share prices

Don't be confused or put off by the dollar value of a company's individual shares. I've heard lots of people say that Macquarie Bank must be a good investment because its share price is so high – above $120 – compared to, say, the Commonwealth Bank at $74, or something else that sells for 1c. Yes, Macquarie has been a good investment, but there is a fallacy at the heart of this way of speaking. The fallacy is a variety of 'money illusion'.

The price of an individual share depends on the number of shares that have been issued. (In other words, how many shares has the company divided itself up into?) A company worth $100 in total, and with only one share issued, will have a higher share price that a billion-dollar company with ten billion shares. But I'd rather have a big stake in the second company than the first, all else being equal.

The term 'market capitalisation' or 'market cap' refers to the total value of the equity of a company. This is the total value available to shareholders after all debts and expenses and taxes are paid. It is calculated by multiplying the share price by the number of shares. In the above example, the first company has a $100 market cap, the second one a $1 billion market cap.

Another way of thinking about this is to compare a single $80 share with a parcel of twenty $4 shares. Both the individual $80 share and the parcel of four shares are worth $80 on the market; neither is better or worse. Based on the shares' risk and return, the market has valued the share and the parcel at the same level. What's important in this valuation is not the nominal share price but how it is likely to change over time – based on the performance of the company, the level of dividends, and the associated level of risk.

THE ALL ORDINARIES

On the ASX, the **All Ordinaries**, or **All Ords**, which I quote on the ABC News every night, reflects the price movements of the largest 500 listed stocks – not 'all'. The companies that make up the index are selected on the basis of their market capitalisation. Although the ASX actually has more than 2000 listed companies, the majority are small and inactively traded, and hence less likely to have an impact on the overall market.

Takeovers

Takeover bids are part of the daily cut and thrust of the share market. A bidding company typically aims to buy all the shares in a target company – so there are fewer loose ends, and so the acquirer has greater control. If the takeover proceeds, therefore, investors in the target company must say farewell to their old shares. But they do so with compensations. If a bid is cash-only, then investors in the target company are offered cash in exchange for their shares. If a bid is scrip-only, then investors are offered shares in the acquiring company. Investors can choose to hold on to those shares or to sell them on the market. Sometimes investors are offered cash, sometimes scrip, and sometimes a mixture of both.

Not all takeovers are welcomed, but investors in target companies often end up with cash or shares worth more than their original investment. The cash can be reinvested. The shares you receive will give you a stake, in most cases, in what is a stronger company.

The original shareholders in the acquiring company may not do so well. In a scrip offer, for example, they may face a diminution in the value of their shares. Also, experience has shown that takeovers are often launched for the wrong reasons, including executive egos. Be wary, therefore, of companies with aggressive takeover plans.

*We don't like acquisition machines, management that
are out there doing big acquisitions all the time, because
we know that those things often end in tears.*

STEPHEN ARNOLD,
Aoris Investment Management

The *Corporations Law*, the corporate regulators and the ASX
all apply rules that are aimed at protecting smaller investors during
takeovers. The protections include rules about disclosure and
avoiding predatory conduct.

Key concepts in share investment

If you spend any time with share investors or at the ASX, or if you
read the financial press, you will encounter some pieces of financial jargon over and over. Here is a primer on some of the most
important terms in share investing.

Initial public offerings (IPOs)

A company undergoing an IPO or float is like the public 'reveal'
of a new invention. After the IPO, the company's shares trade for
the first time. When a company is preparing to float, it issues a
prospectus that sets out all the relevant financial details and risks
involved. Investors use the prospectus to apply for shares.

Shares are offered to institutions and to the clients of the
brokers who've been appointed to market the issue. High-profile
floats for well-known private companies may also be advertised
in the media.

Not all floats are winners. In fact, the majority lose money in
their early years. Take, for example, the retail group Myer Holdings, which was floated in November 2009, three years after
being bought from Coles Myer by private equity interests. After
an aggressive marketing campaign that targeted the store's loyal

cardholding customers, the new shares were issued at $4.10. On their first day of trading they slumped to $3.75. A year later, investors who took part in the float were still waiting for a profit. Today, the shares are trading at around 43 cents, and the very future of the company is a hot issue.

UNMARKETABLE HOLDINGS

Patrick Hatch, writing in *The Sydney Morning Herald* in 2018, revealed that around one in two Myer shareholders were trapped with parcels of stock too small to sell.

'Shareholdings are considered "unmarketable" when their value dips below $500, because they are difficult to sell and the cost of doing so can eat up much of their sale value.'

According to the company's 2017 annual report, 17,150 Myer shareholders had unmarketable parcels – when the share price was 77 cents. As the share price fell further, the number of shareholders with unsellable holdings grew.

Myer was under pressure to buy back the unmarketable holdings, notwithstanding the high number of shareholders involved.

What about surfwear and leisure retailer Billabong, another iconic brand? Billabong floated in 2000 at an issue price of $2.30. In its early years the stock did well, trading above $9. Then the company's outlook soured, and the share price slumped. In 2017, Billabong shares fell 40 per cent in light of poor trading results and high debt levels. In 2018, the slump continued, until the company was taken over. Some shareholders who bought in 2008 saw their shares fall by more than 92 per cent. That means a $10,000 investment would have turned into $800.

Let's have a look now at how some other famous shares have performed since they were first listed on the market.

As part of its privatisation, Telstra (the old Telecom) was sold in three stages or 'tranches' of shares. In the first phase (1997) the shares were priced at $3.30 each. The second phase (1999) coincided with the dotcom boom, and the shares went to market at $7.40 – and soon reached an all-time high of $9.16. After the dotcom bust, the share price fell substantially; the third tranche was sold directly to the Future Fund. At 30 June 2019, the share price was $3.86.

The Commonwealth Bank has a better story than Telstra's. In 1991, CBA shares first traded at $5.40. Since that time, the shares have gone up 1350 per cent. Along the way, the bank has paid substantial dividends. On 30 June 2019, the share price was $83.36.

And CSL, the star performer of the ASX, is a better story still. Originally floated at $2.30 per share in 1994 (or 76 cents in adjusted terms, allowing for a series of share buybacks), the price as of 30 June 2019 was $216.07. An initial investment of $10,000 would now be worth over $2.8 million, plus the $140,000 of dividends paid since the float.

If you consider yourself an investor rather than a speculator, then you need to research the company's vital statistics before you invest in an IPO. At the time of the Myer float, many analysts warned that the shares were overvalued. You did not need to be a financial whiz to see that the forecasts of future performance were optimistic and that this optimism was reflected in the issue price.

A lot of hope, and some greed, rides on share floats. In reality, it's not unusual for investors to lose money on one in every two IPOs. The ASX website offers a table of recently listed stocks that can help you gauge the prospects of IPOs.

> **INSIGHTS FROM MY FRIEND TOM HART**
>
> 'As Kenny Rogers sang in "The Gambler" – Kerry Packer's favourite song – "You gotta know when to hold 'em, know when to fold 'em!" Kerry knew.
>
> I bought CSL shares at the float and when they got to $11 I decided to sell enough to cover the cost of purchase, so I effectively had the rest for nothing. Clever Tom!?
>
> How could they keep on growing in value?
>
> I realised my mistake when they got to $30 and bought them back. Now they are effectively worth nearly $600 in pre-dilution terms and I'm $500,000 in front.
>
> Investing is a gamble and as David Walsh says in his auto-biography, *A Bone of Fact*, "If you gamble without an edge, you're a silly duffer."
>
> The edge in share market investing is information plus experience.'

Rights issue

Like an IPO, a rights issue is a way for a company to raise funds by issuing new shares. In a rights issue, the shares are issued, usually at a discount to the market price, to existing shareholders in proportion to the number of shares they hold. For example, you might be offered one share for every four shares you currently have. You then have the right, but not the obligation, to take up the new shares. In some cases, the rights may be sold on the stock market.

Bonus shares

You don't often see bonus issues these days. There used to be lots of them before people caught on to the fact that they're not a bonus at all, but simple a way of splitting the company's value into smaller pieces. These days companies only ever do it to get the price of their shares down, because they think more people will buy them if they're $5 instead of $500 each. Maybe they're right. Anyway, the way it works is that the new shares are issued free to existing shareholders, usually in a ratio to the number of shares already held. For example, a one-for-five bonus issue means shareholders receive one bonus share for every five ordinary shares they already hold.

Share buyback

A share buyback is exactly what it sounds like: a company buys back some of its shares and then cancels them. In a way, it's the opposite of a share split, or bonus issue: the company wants to reduce the number of shares on issue to boost the value of each one, and they generally use buybacks as a way to tax-effectively give money back to shareholders. That's because the cash is effectively distributed as a capital gain instead of a taxable dividend, and it's mostly done by companies that don't have a lot of franking credits, in turn because they get a lot of their profits from overseas and don't pay much Australian company tax. There are numerous types of buybacks; the most straightforward is an 'equal access' buyback. Shareholders are offered an opportunity to consider the offer, which is to buy back the same percentage of their ordinary shares. A 'selective' buyback is one in which identical offers are not made to every shareholder – for example, offers are made to only some of the shareholders. Other types of buybacks include employee share scheme buybacks and on-market buybacks.

MARKET BUBBLES AND HOW TO SPOT THEM

- Bubbles are classic examples of markets being driven by people who've lost touch with reality.
- The first true bubbles were in novel markets, such as the market for tulips and for new types of company.
- In those bubbles, there was unbridled enthusiasm – very few people were voicing scepticism about the market prices – and there were few 'reference prices' (such as prices from history and from similar markets) against which prices could be compared. Hence prices got a long way from a realistic level.
- Today, how can you tell if you are in a bubble? If the market is not novel, if there are reference prices, if people are saying it is a bubble, then it is very likely not a bubble.

FAMOUS BUBBLES

The Tulip Mania (1634–37), the Mississippi Bubble (1718–20), the South Sea Bubble (1719–21), the Poseidon Boom (1969–70), New York stock exchange (2006–09), NASDAQ and the dot-com bubble (1994–2002), Japanese shares (1982–92) and Bitcoin (2014–?)

THE POSEIDON BOOM

During the Vietnam War, demand for nickel surged. When employees of a major Canadian nickel supplier went on strike, a worldwide shortage followed. In Western Australia, Ken Shirley found promising nickel sources; in 1969, news of the find spread. Shares in Shirley's company, Poseidon, skyrocketed.

The rise in Poseidon also inflated the share prices of other mining companies. Unscrupulous opportunists rushed to list on the exchange and investors poured their money in. Mining stocks peaked in January 1970, then immediately crashed. People saw through the hollow promises of the new businesses, and Poseidon itself was shown to be much less of a prospect than first thought. Its nickel was of a lower grade, and the extraction costs were higher.

Having risen from 50c to $35 on the first reports of the nickel sample, Poseidon peaked at $280 in February 1970. It had risen by 34,900 per cent. In 1976, it delisted. The aftermath of the boom led to the creation of Australia's modern companies and securities legislation.

Buying shares

There is no guarantee that you will profit from investing in shares. They may lose some or all of their value. But on average shares are often a good investment. Dividends are not guaranteed in the same way as interest from a government bond or bank term deposit, but they do provide a relatively stable income stream from big companies like banks with mature businesses and secure earnings. A portfolio of stocks with a high dividend yield can suit retirees and anyone who depends on income from their investments.

The market price of the additional risk of shares (the equity risk premium) is around 3 per cent. So if you can get a 6 per cent return from cash or government bonds (that seems high today, but is around the long-term average), you should expect a total return from shares of around 9 per cent.

Investors who don't depend on income may choose to reinvest their dividends in more shares to gain the benefits of compounding. This is very important for the returns you can achieve in the long run. Some companies offer dividend reinvestment plans, often at a discount to the current share price, which has the added benefit of not requiring a fee for brokerage.

TIPS FOR SELECTING SHARES

It is often a good idea to start close to home. Do you know and respect the company you work for? What about the places you shop? Have you had really good service from a company? It's a good idea to start with companies you know, like JB Hi-Fi and Harvey Norman.

It's the little things that often tell you whether a company is well run. Does it pay attention to customer service? Does it differentiate itself in the market? Is it committed to quality? Does it mess up basic details? If you haven't had personal dealings with a company you are going to invest in, do some research. Companies produce prospectuses and annual reports that contain essential information designed to help you understand them as an investment.

Most professional share market investors rely on some form of 'fundamental analysis' to research the financial health of listed companies. Factors such as sustained growth in sales and earnings, return on assets and shareholders' equity, the level of debt to equity and capital management are all put under the microscope.

These concepts are discussed in more detail in the sections that follow. By using actual figures from the most recent financial year and estimates for the current and future years, analysts calculate the theoretical value of a company's shares. This is referred to as intrinsic, or fundamental, value. Some professionals use a qualitative approach, focusing on aspects of the underlying business, its trading environment and its management. Others use a quantitative approach that relies on a computer-based statistical and mathematical analysis of shares.

An understanding of the business, its prospects and value is crucial if you want to maximise your chance of investment success, but so is an appreciation of price and timing. Warren Buffett stresses the importance of buying shares in great businesses at a fair price. Timing is crucial here; we will return to this later.

COMPANIES COME AND GO

A glance at the top 100 Australian companies of twenty years ago, or even ten years ago, highlights the fact that companies come and go, and that few beat the market for extended periods. Great companies sometimes go through lengthy periods of underperformance or poor management; some are taken over and others just fail and disappear from the market.

Value investing

'Value investing' involves searching for shares that are underpriced according to a relevant ratio or a measure of fundamental value. I don't really like terms like value investing, because they're not really informative, and I don't think anyone should, or wants to, buy an asset for more than it's worth. Any investor, no matter what term they use to describe themselves, wants to buy something cheap. If a stock is worth more than the market price, then it is no doubt a good buy. But value investing isn't everything, and it is not enough as the basis for a comprehensive investment strategy. Some companies that don't look cheap on standard measures are still good investments. Pure value investing is too restrictive; the most dogged value investors miss out of lots of opportunities. They miss out on lots of great stocks that are correctly priced. Over recent years, value investing has underperformed compared to 'growth investing'. Growth investing, in short, means buying expensive stocks and watching them get more expensive. It's been a good investment strategy in recent years because a lot of expensive stocks have been getting even more expensive, confounding the 'value investors' waiting for them to come unstuck.

My top ten tips for investing in shares

1. Diversity is your friend. Unless you really know a company, each investment shouldn't be more than 10 per cent of your share portfolio, and shares should be around 60 per cent of your total investments, although if you're young and just starting out, it's okay to have nothing but shares.

2. You or your adviser should review your share portfolio at least six-monthly, preferably quarterly. Which shares are worth keeping and which ones should be discarded? And most importantly, don't discard the companies you like simply because they have gone up, unless they have become very expensive (according to the ratios – it's not necessarily expensive if the profit has increased with the share price).

3. Don't hold on to a losing stock just because you don't want to admit you made a bad call. Sentimentality and investing don't mix.

4. Timing is important. The time at which you buy is just as important, if not more so, than the time at which you sell.

5. Keep a watchlist of shares you might be interested in buying when the time is right.

6. The corporate reporting season, that comes twice a year – after the end of the financial year and the six-month mark – is a good time to think about your share portfolio and to single out which shares to buy and which to sell. The things to look for in results are consistency and delivering on promises.

7. Your portfolio should include some international exposure, but remember that a lot of Australian companies are really international ones that happen to be based here – for example, BHP and CSL.

8. Benjamin Graham (Warren Buffett's mentor) said that 'in the short run the stock is a voting machine, but in the long it's a weighing machine.' He meant that the short-term fluctuations are about market psychology and herd behaviour, but in the long run quality wins out. In other words, investing for the short term is for speculators – true investing is long term.

9. There are different ways to measure value. The most common is the share price divided by earnings, or profit, per share, called the price-earnings ratio, or PE. Usually it's around fifteen times; less than ten is cheap, more than twenty is getting expensive, although a fast-growing business might look expensive using the PE, but is actually cheap, because in a year or two the PE ratio will be below ten.

10. Remember Warren Buffett's Rule No. 1: Don't lose money. And his Rule No. 2: Don't forget Rule No. 1. Everyone loses money sometimes, but what Buffett is referring to is your mindset. Don't be frivolous. Don't go into an investment with a cavalier attitude. Be informed. Do your homework.

SHARE STRATEGIES FOR BUFFETT-STYLE RETURNS
- Invest for the long term (when that suits your horizon).
- Reinvest dividends and interest, to take advantage of compounding.
- Care about the underlying businesses.
- Favour high-performing companies that retain and reinvest profits rather than distribute them as dividends.

KEY INSIGHT
If a company is the best place for wealth creation, then it's best to reinvest dividends in the company.

A good investor buys stocks when they are cheap and unloved, holds on when a good company is temporarily out of favour, and sells when a stock is no longer good value.

Inexperienced investors tend to do the opposite – they buy when the smart money has already pushed up the share price and sell in a panic when the smart money has moved on and the share price has collapsed, without ever understanding what a stock is really worth.

Share diversification

Owning shares in a variety of sectors and geographic locations means that a slump in one part of the economy won't wipe out all your profits.

You may have looked at a stock that has gone up spectacularly, and thought: 'Gee, if only I'd had all my money in that one.' CSL springs to mind: as we've seen, if you'd invested $10,000 when CSL floated twenty-five years ago, that would now be worth

$2.8 million. But you didn't, did you? You couldn't possibly have known what would happen.

It's true that diversification tends to water down your returns, but that's only with the benefit of hindsight. You can't know ahead of time which of your investments are going to be the best ones, nor can you know for sure which industries and which countries will do best. It's far better to spread your bets.

Bank and resources stocks accounted for around 40 per cent of the Australian market in 2018–19, which means its fortunes were dominated by these two market sectors. Close to half of the total sales revenue that comes into ASX-listed companies is actually off-shore earnings, and many of the new stocks being listed these days, especially technology ones, are globally focused, so it's possible to get a good geographical spread for your portfolio without leaving home, as it were. But of course some of the best international companies aren't listed here: Amazon, Google, Microsoft and Alibaba are worth considering as well.

And don't forget that companies are kind of fund managers, too: they take capital and invest it in assets to make money. BHP, for example, manages a range of investments, all of them mines and oil wells. There is no strong dividing line between companies and funds, or between company managers and fund managers. They are parts of a continuum, and the same principles apply to companies and mutual funds.

Of course, that doesn't mean you could put all your money in BHP and say it's a diversified investment. It might own a whole lot of mines, but it's one management team and one board of directors, with one approach. Diversification also means investing in a few different groups of people.

A fund manager I know, who has made about 25 per cent per annum return for a while, invests in around thirty businesses, which he reckons is enough to achieve the diversification he needs.

Contrast this with investing just in BHP: there is diversification across assets, but not across asset types; all BHP has are its mines and wells, and they produce broadly the same types of products.

It used to be possible to get quite a lot of diversification by investing in 'conglomerates', which are companies that operate in a whole lot of unconnected businesses, but they don't really exist anymore. It's because professional investors prefer to do their own diversifying, thanks very much, and don't need directors and managers to do it for them. In fact, the only true conglomerate left in the Australian market is Wesfarmers, and it often talks about having a valuable 'conglomerate licence' – that is, a licence from the market to stay a conglomerate. In fact, the main reason Wesfarmers has divested Coles is so it keeps the conglomerate licence – its retail businesses had become too dominant.

So these days most companies 'stick to their knitting', under strict instructions from investors, mainly doing one thing or a narrow set of similar things.

The idea is that diversification can still happen – but at the fund manager level and the individual investor level, not at the company level. And, so the logic goes, if companies stay focused, then there is more flexibility about how people can diversify (diversification levels and asset allocations are no longer fixed by conglomerate structures), and capital can go to the best uses, which is beneficial for everyone.

Foreign shares

Buying an asset somewhere else, whether it's company shares or anything else, involves taking two risks instead of one: the thing itself and the currency. The price of the asset you buy could stay unchanged, but you could still make money if the currency of the place you bought it in goes up. Obviously if both the price of the asset and the currency go up, you could make a lot of money, and conversely if they both go down you could lose a lot.

'GOOD' AND 'BAD' SHARES

My friend's brother, let's call him John, recently announced that he was entering the stock market for the first time. He told me he planned to buy some shares, and in particular some 'good' shares. After I gave him a quizzical look, he explained that 'good' shares were ones that were less expensive and had low risk but high returns.

I wished him well, and told him one of Warren Buffett's favourite sayings: 'It's far better to buy a wonderful company at a fair price than a fair company at a wonderful price.'

In other words, don't get too caught up on price. Sometimes you have to pay what seems like a high price for a great company, but that's better than buying a cheap lemon. It's just like buying a car, in a way – you get what you pay for.

For that reason, I think you need to approach this carefully. In a way, you'd be making two investments at once and should approach it that way. That is, you have to understand two investments – the company you're buying into, if it's foreign shares, and the currency. (Note also that foreign shares don't attract franking credits.)

To be honest, I think currencies are not great investments and should be avoided. That's because so much can go wrong. A currency is a relative price, not an absolute one, which means it is only expressed in terms of the other currency. That means you can lose out from investing in, say, India if either the rupee goes down or the Australian dollar goes up, and there are a huge number of things that make those things happen, which means currencies are notoriously difficult to predict.

Far better, in my view, is to get direct currency risk out of the equation. There are two ways to do this: either buy shares in international companies listed on the ASX, or buy into managed funds that invest in international shares, many of which are also listed on the ASX.

You can't entirely avoid currency risk, because the profits of the companies and the returns of the funds tend to fluctuate according to what the currencies do. But at least they've got experts managing their currency risk and in many cases they hedge the risk, which simply means they use futures markets to offset it by locking in a certain exchange rate.

Sometimes you can choose between a hedged and unhedged fund, in which case I think you should always go for the hedged fund, so you are removing currency risk from the equation. Let's face it – it's already hard to get investing in companies and funds right without adding the extra complication of investing in a currency.

The other risk to keep an eye on with international investing is sovereign risk. This basically means the risk that the country concerned will change the rules in some way so that the company you've invested in can't make the profits it – and you – thought it was going to make. Sometimes that can mean full confiscation of the company's assets, but not often.

And the trouble with sovereign risk is that sometimes it can come out of the blue. For example, in 2018 investors in Turkey suffered huge losses because the newly re-elected President Recep Tayyip Erdoğan picked a fight with President Donald Trump of the United States, who promptly imposed sanctions and tariffs against Turkey. The currency fell 30 per cent in a hurry, which meant every investment in Turkey fell by the same amount. European banks that had lent money to Turkey, and Turkish companies, all lost a fortune, so even though there wasn't an issue of sovereign risk with Italy, France and Spain, investors in those banks all suffered sovereign risk.

THE ASX OFFERS INTERNATIONAL EXPOSURE

The ASX can get you a long way towards where
you want to go.

- Key Australian companies are global, such as CSL,
  Cochlear and BHP.
- There are about 150 companies based overseas – in
  countries such as the US, UK, Israel and China – but
  listed on the ASX.
- Listed funds give access to foreign shares in specific
  regions and sectors.
- And with the ASX, you can use Australian dollars,
  thereby reducing currency risk.

Having said all that, expanding your investment horizons by buying shares in companies that operate overseas, whether through a fund or directly, is a good idea. Australia is a great country and is the current world record holder for length of time without a recession, yet we haven't got much of a technology sector – or manufacturing anymore, for that matter.

And also, global growth is not always, or even usually, synchronised – that is, some countries do well at the same time as others do badly, so spreading your investments around can smooth out the volatility of your portfolio.

If you are able to build a share portfolio, what proportion of it should be international shares? No less than 20 per cent, I'd say. Obviously, since Australia represents less than 2 per cent of the global economy, you could justify having more than 20 per cent of your portfolio invested in the other 98 per cent, but most people don't feel comfortable going that far – understandably. We know Australia best, and it's always advisable to invest in things you know.

Ways to buy shares

For many years, stockbrokers dominated the buying and selling of shares. The big names when I first encountered the stock market were firms like Potter Partners and J.B. Were and Ord Minnett. If you wanted to buy a particular stock, you instructed your broker to make the purchase on your behalf. And just as often – actually more often, to be honest – the broker would call you with recommendations and tips, trying to get you do something, and therefore pay them a commission.

These days, however, things have changed. Traditional 'retail' stockbrokers are rapidly disappearing. Most 'human' stockbrokers now deal mostly with institutions and high-wealth investors. When the rest of us want to buy shares, we do it via online brokers (or indirectly via financial planners and fund managers).

The dominance of online brokers – organisations like Macquarie Online Trading, nabtrade and CommSec – has had important impacts. Unlike the old brokerages, the online brokers provide much less guidance and research, and fewer tips. 'Human' brokers used to provide ideas about where to invest. Online brokers do this to some extent, but mainly their service is transactional – an 'execution only' service. You tell them what you want to buy, and they put through the trade.

One implication of this is that there is a stronger onus on you to know what you are going to buy. Another implication is anthropological. My friend (the one who didn't like her accountant) shared these thoughts about dealing with stockbrokers: 'I'm in an online forum for women who want to be savvier with their money. Another member of the forum recently bought her first shares – and she did so through an online broker as it felt less confronting and more accessible. I would prefer it that way as well, so I could avoid the patronising attitude of moneyed men that I see displayed so often by accountants I deal with. I can see a lot of appeal in online brokers.'

Buying through online brokers can also be less confronting for people who have less experience of financial markets and who have less money to invest. But everyone needs to have their wits about them when buying shares through any route. And as always, we all need to pay close attention to fees, and to the fine print, and to the range of services that are offered.

All brokers can trade shares, but not all of them offer access to more-complex instruments such as options, futures, warrants and contracts for difference (CFDs). You need to ask about this. Also, if you are an experienced investor or trader, you might want a wide range of products, trading tools and charts. And as a new investor, you might value educational tools and ease of use.

Online brokers often require you to open a cash-management account linked to their trading platform before you begin trading.

When using an online broker, you have to know what you want to buy. If you are unsure of what you want to buy – perhaps you like the idea of buying in a particular industry but don't know which company to buy – then you need to do some research, or ask a financial adviser or a 'human' stockbroker.

Margin loans and gearing

Gearing, which means borrowing money to invest, is a legitimate investment strategy, but risky, especially with shares (less so with property, because the price doesn't move around as much, or as quickly). By borrowing money to invest, you increase the expected return of your investment portfolio, and you also increase the risk and volatility (fluctuations in value) of your portfolio. This means gearing is a strategy only suited to those investors with a high tolerance for fluctuations in the value of their portfolio.

Online brokers	Fee for $15,000 trade (Australian shares) as of 30 June 2019
SelfWealth	$9.50
HSBC	$19.95
Macquarie Online Trading	$19.95
ANZ	$19.95
Bendigo Invest Direct	$19.95
nabtrade	$14.95
CommSec	$29.95

With gearing, there will be much greater losses of capital in the event of severe market downturns, which do happen from time to time.

'Margin loans' are lines of credit without fixed terms and with interest-only repayments. With a margin loan, you can borrow money to invest in shares, managed funds or fixed-interest securities, using the investments you buy as security for the loan. The lender, usually a bank or financier associated with a broker, specifies a list of acceptable securities.

Lenders typically offer up to a maximum of 70 per cent of the value of the underlying shares, referred to as the loan-to-valuation ratio (LVR). The borrower must deposit enough cash or shares to make up the difference, or margin. For example, if you have $30,000 in savings or existing shares and borrow an additional $70,000, giving you a total share market investment of $100,000, you have an LVR of 70 per cent.

INAPPROPRIATE ADVICE: GEARING

George sought advice about his investments. The financial adviser recommended that George sell his existing investments and borrow to buy other (geared) investments, and borrow an additional amount to buy additional agribusiness investments.

The Credit and Investments Ombudsman (CIO) found that the advice on the geared investments was appropriate as this advice suited George's investment goals, risk profile and time frame. However, the CIO found that the advice on the agribusiness investments was not appropriate as George would have met his goals with the geared investments, and did not need to take the additional risk of the further investments.

The CIO also found that the adviser did not establish a reasonable basis for recommending the additional agribusiness investments, and that the investments were unlikely to be of benefit to George. The CIO concluded that the adviser provided George with inappropriate advice. The adviser's licensee offered compensation of $174,647, which George accepted.

Source: Credit and Investments Ombudsman, 2018

Gearing up with a margin loan has the potential to magnify profits if your shares go up in price, but the reverse can also happen. The market value of the portfolio is monitored daily, and if it falls below the LVR plus a 5 per cent buffer, the lender makes a margin call. You then have twenty-four hours to stump up cash or sell shares to restore the LVR to the agreed value. Margin calls can come as a shock and are definitely not for the faint-hearted!

Margin loans tend to be more popular during bull markets, when share prices are high and rising. But everyone should exercise caution with this type of investing. A sharp correction in prices can result in a series of margin calls that force you to sell your shares at the worst possible time. Borrowers need sufficient income to cover interest rate rises and enough cash reserves to cover margin calls to avoid selling shares on short notice into a falling market. In general, gearing is for people who have a high risk appetite. Novice investors should steer clear of margin loans.

Final words about the share market

The 2017 ASX Australian Investor Study found that Australia had more than 11 million investors, most investors had a long-term investment horizon, and shares were by far the most commonly held exchange-traded investment.

According to the study, the Australian share market had outperformed other developed share markets globally. Trading volumes had increased 23 per cent over the twelve months to March, and continued to grow. Domestic equity market capitalisation reached a historic high, of $1.8 trillion. Investing was becoming more common among young people; the proportion of 18- to 24-year-olds investing had doubled over five years from 10 to 20 per cent.

Ownership of international shares had also increased: nearly 8 per cent of the adult population say that they directly held shares listed on an international financial exchange, up from 5 per cent in 2014.

Around 60 per cent of all investors used some form of professional advice (from a financial planner, a full-service stockbroker, an accountant or a solicitor) to guide their investment decisions. And the remaining 40 per cent of investors? I'm not sure what they were doing. Probably some of them were just dabbling in the market to a modest extent. Others would have gone deeper, and a significant proportion of these would have been confident that they knew what they were doing. But I'm sure a substantial number were just flying by the seat of their pants.

Investing in the share market can be a lot of fun. There are so many fascinating businesses, often companies you use every day, like Coles and Woolworths, or your bank, or perhaps even Facebook and Google on the New York Stock Exchange. And there are lots of small start-ups that are trying to do something interesting, to disrupt an existing business. Investing in start-ups can be hit and miss, but it can also be fun. For example, one of my small investments is in a company called Collaborate Corporation, which is trying to get a peer-to-peer car and caravan rental business off the ground. I'm not getting rich from it, that's for sure, but it's an interesting ride. Another disruptor that I've invested in is called Pushpay Holdings, an Australian company that is selling an app that helps American churches collect donations online instead of taking the plate around on Sunday – because no one has any cash anymore! And this one is going really well. And even if you don't take the plunge, looking through all the exotic options on the ASX is enjoyable in itself, and maybe you'll find something that takes your fancy – and makes you a lot of money!

9

Managed Funds, Index Funds & Other Funds

I N THIS CHAPTER I EXPLORE A VARIETY OF DIFFERENT types of investment funds that are broadly grouped as 'managed funds'. Today, such funds are incredibly important. Their use is widespread – your financial adviser is likely to recommend one or more to you – and they come in many different forms: listed or unlisted, actively or passively managed, specialising in property or some other type of asset, and operating through trusts or companies or with some form of direct ownership.

Despite the diversity of funds, they all have important things in common. A 'managed fund' is exactly what the name suggests: a fund or investment vehicle that is managed by an investment specialist, usually through a structure into which multiple investors can put their money. The manager selects investments that reflect the fund's stated goals and scope, and its investment philosophy. A managed fund can invest in shares, property, fixed-interest securities, alternative assets or a combination of these.

Basically, when you invest through a managed fund, you're 'hiring' someone to invest your money for you. Broadly there are two ways to do it: either a pooled investment fund, or what's called a 'managed account', where ownership of the assets stays with you but someone else manages the portfolio.

A lot of people choose a managed account for tax reasons. On the other hand, pooling is better if the amount of money is not very big. That's because investors in a managed fund can get access to investments that are often only available to institutions or high-wealth individuals with lots of money. Pooling your money gives you the opportunity to invest in large-scale investments such as a shopping centre or office block that might otherwise be too big to digest.

Investors in a pooled fund are issued 'units' according to how much money they invest. For example, a person investing $1000 in a managed fund with a unit price of $1 will receive 1000 units in the fund. If the value of the investments held in the managed fund goes up, the unit price increases in tandem. Conversely, if the investments fall in value, the unit price also falls.

As well as investors receiving a return on their investment because of changes in the unit price, most managed funds pay regular distributions, usually twice a year but sometimes monthly for funds that are aimed at retirees seeking income to live on. These are made up of the income that has been earnt from the fund's investments, plus any capital gains from assets that have been sold. The returns may also include currency gains as a result of movements in exchange rates relative to the Australian dollar, and tax credits such as franking credits attached to dividends paid by underlying share investments. As an investor, you are also liable for tax on any income and capital gains in proportion to the number of units you own.

For example, a managed fund made up of Australian shares will receive dividends from holding those shares over the year.

At a specified date (such as 30 June) the managed fund will pay the value of the dividends to the unit holders in the form of a distribution.

Managed funds can invest in a single asset class, such as Australian shares, or in multiple asset classes. A 'balanced' fund might invest in a range of asset classes, including Australian shares, international shares, listed property trusts, fixed interest investments and cash investments within the one fund. The experience of an investor in a managed fund will closely follow the performance of the types of assets in the fund. If the asset class performs well, the unit holders will, too.

A single managed-fund investment can provide access to a well-diversified underlying portfolio for a relatively small outlay of capital. An investment in an Australian share fund, for example, might provide access to a portfolio of fifty companies or more. For a few thousand dollars you can buy units in a fund with exposure to the top 200 Australian shares or a portfolio of global listed property. An investment in a balanced fund can provide diversification across a broad range of asset classes and investments.

This level of diversification can be particularly suitable for investors starting out with a small amount of money. With a $2000 initial investment, for example, there is no cost-effective way to build a well-diversified portfolio by directly purchasing shares of fifty Australian companies. But a managed fund can easily provide this level of diversification. Managed funds can also allow investors to access international shares, private equity, overseas property and other asset classes that are hard to invest in directly as an individual.

Fees

How much should you pay for this service – for 'hiring' someone to manage a portfolio of investments for you? Well, there's a wide range of fees, but the two key ones are 'base fee' and 'performance fee'.

The base fee is taken from your account each month what-ever happens, and while it can range from 0.5 per cent to 1.5 per cent, it's usually somewhere in the middle. That means if you've given the fund manager $100,000, you're paying him or her $83 per month; if it's $1 million, which is what a lot of people have to invest in retirement, the fee is at least $830 a month.

Is that reasonable? Only you can decide that, but personally – I don't think it is. For a start, it costs almost no more to manage $1 million than to manage $100,000, so the extra is pure cream, or, to put it another way, those with more money are subsidising those with less.

My other problem with those percentage fees is that the fee obviously increases with the amount of money in the account, and on average that is going to increase much faster than the fund manager's costs or the inflation rate, especially if you are contrib-uting regularly to the fund. Even if you don't put more money in, investment returns tend, on average, to be greater than inflation – that's the whole point of investing!

And then there's the performance fee. That's where the manager takes a large percentage – usually 10 to 20 per cent – of any return over a benchmark, often but not always the ASX share index. So if the performance fee is 20 per cent and the benchmark is the ASX 200 index, and the manager produces a return of 10 per cent when the index went up 5 per cent, then the manager gets an extra 1 per cent on top of the base fee (20 per cent of the difference between 5 and 10).

It's really important to keep an eye on the benchmark with these performance fee arrangements, because sometimes it is very low – even zero! I once interviewed a fund manager because he had announced that due to poor performance he was cancelling his base fee, which I thought was an unusually magnanimous gesture. But then it turned out that his performance fee, which he was continuing to take, was 20 per cent of anything over zero. In other words, he was charging a fifth of any return he got. I actually think that's not a bad way to go. At least the manager only gets paid if you get a return – he doesn't just keep getting paid no matter what.

But it all goes to show that fees are important and variable. You should never feel shy about asking what the fees are and then calculating what that means in dollar terms for you. If it feels too high, it probably is, and you should say so. It's OK to say no, and to shop around. After all, the fee is the one thing you can control: how the investments perform is up to the gods of the market.

The managed fund industry

Australia's managed fund industry is huge. According to statistics published on the website of US managed funds industry site the Investment Company Institute, Australia has one of the biggest managed fund industries in the world, thanks to the mandatory superannuation system. At the start of 2018 the value of the assets invested in Australian managed funds was just over $3.4 trillion. Given our population of 25 million, that equates to $136,000 invested in managed funds for every man, woman and child in Australia.

Today, there are thousands of managed funds available in Australia. The largest fund managers measure their 'funds under management' in the tens of billions of dollars.

A good fund provides the highest return for a given level of risk or the lowest risk for a given level of return.

AUSTRALIA'S FUNDS MANAGEMENT INDUSTRY

Australia's funds management industry is the largest in the Asia-Pacific region and the sixth largest in the world, according to the survey produced by Washington-based Investment Company Institute (ICI). The survey also found Australia was:

- the fourth largest in alternative assets under management
- the eighth largest foreign exchange market
- the ninth largest stock market measured by free-float market capitalisation
- the tenth largest market for international and domestic debt securities combined.

Fund managers

When you invest in a managed fund, the person actively managing your money is a full-time investment professional. He or she is a specialist who chooses different investments – stocks, bonds, other securities and investment vehicles – and bundles them together into funds.

Fund managers think about the risk, return, maturity and liquidity of the menu of available investments. A good fund manager gets the basics right, and applies skill and intelligence to the task of picking investments. Part scientist, part magician, the best fund managers can achieve materially higher returns consistently over time. And, as I've already emphasised, every percentage point counts.

And one of the key things a fund manager can do that you mostly can't is visit the company and look the CEO in the eye, as well as inspect businesses. The best fund managers I speak to visit hundreds of companies every year and reject 90 per cent of them, but they all say there's only so much you can know about a business from your office or home: you can't really get a feel for it unless you go to it and eyeball the management.

WHAT MAKES A GOOD FUND MANAGER?

A great 'fundie':

- has the highest integrity
- is usually a bit of a 'nerd' – enjoys crunching numbers and doesn't go out much
- has a hunger and a passion to serve investors' interests
- has a good track record over a number of years – they have endured at least one cycle of boom and bust
- has 'skin in the game' – his or her own money is in the fund
- has a clear and deliberate investment strategy, covering the next three to five years, and doesn't rely on luck or gut feel
- cares about the underlying investments
- is not narrowly focused on a particular company, sector or mode of investing
- is more focused on capital preservation and capital growth than on high dividends and high annual returns
- invests in businesses that are highly profitable but pay low or no dividends
- doesn't trade too frequently; frequent trading generates high transaction costs that eat away at returns
- has a fair and appropriate approach to fees and charges
- has personal resilience in the bad times and realism in the boom times
- is prepared to burn some shoe leather and visit lots of companies.

SKIN IN THE GAME: PAUL MOORE OF PM CAPITAL

'I've been the portfolio manager of our global fund since inception and I'm the biggest investor in the fund. I have a team of very senior portfolio managers who have been with me between ten and twenty years. There are also shareholders in the company and then we have a number of analysts who have been with us obviously for a less period of time and helped with the work we do but they're also shareholders in the business. ... We kind of see ourselves as an owner/operator, what distinguishes us is the fact that we co-invest with our clients in our funds. I think that's our big distinguishing feature. We're typically the largest investor in each of our funds and we think that's really important from an alignment of interest point of view with the shareholders and the unit holders. Also from my point of view to me it's a way of making sure everyone else is part of the business and kind of gets locked into that mentality of being an investor first and always putting the shareholder first.'

You should try to understand the philosophy of your 'fundie': are they conservative, or risk-takers; 'value' or 'growth' investors; followers, or people of pure numbers.

Fund managers often don't think about the capital gains tax implications of what they do. They invest on behalf of a wide range of people with different time horizons and tax arrangements. Use a fundie whose strategies best match your tax circumstances; if you have particular tax issues, think about using a managed account instead of a pooled fund.

All fund managers come with a disclaimer: as I said about superannuation funds, past performance is not indicative of future results. But past performance is all you have to go on. In my experience, if a fund manager has consistently outperformed the market, then there is a good chance they will continue to do so. But there are lots of caveats here. The higher performance could be due to the fundie taking on higher risk, and the higher risk could lead to big swings and large losses. Also, they might have been riding a wave that is now petering out, so it's best, where possible, to get an understanding of how a good performing fund manager has been doing it – by just picking good companies, or by having a lot of money in, say, mining stocks during a mining boom.

Ask questions. What is the fee? Has the fund performed well over a long time frame? How was the performance achieved? Is it able to deal with the inevitable ups and downs of markets? Look at the performance over five to seven years at least. Has there been a big change in strategy or personnel at the fund? One problem is that there aren't many public registers. The company I work for, InvestSMART, provides a free database of all the fees and performances of all the fund managers in Australia.

'Star fundies'
In the 1990s, some high-profile individuals left big institutional fund managers to start their own independent, boutique funds. After the tech wreck of 2000, the trickle of new boutique funds quickly became a flood as 'star' managers set up shop to make their fortunes.

Even when it's plain sailing in the markets, 'star' managers have a tendency to shine brightly for a time and then fade and blend into their surroundings. A number of academic studies have found that boutique managers tend to outperform mainstream fund managers for the first few years. As investors pour money into the new funds, chasing higher returns, the stars lose some of their shine. Their competitive advantage ebbs away because they can no longer find enough outstanding opportunities. After the initial honeymoon period, the returns of most boutique managers tend to revert to the market average.

That's partly because it's harder for a large fund to perform well than a small one: the bigger the fund, the bigger the companies they have to invest in, and big companies, by definition, have a greater influence on the share indices, so the more money you have in them, the more likely it is your performance will match the index.

And star fundies tend to attract a lot of money and grow quickly, which means their performance inevitably returns to the mean – or the index – simply because they have to invest in bigger and bigger companies.

With star fundies, there is an especially high 'key-person risk'. If the fund's outperformance depends on one or two 'investment geniuses', there is every possibility that they will take their talents somewhere else. The best way to guard against that risk is to select a financial planner who knows the fund management market well, has a wide spread of good relationships with fundies, and has the right incentives to look after his or her clients by putting their money into the top-ranking funds.

> *Management changes, like marital changes, are painful,*
> *time-consuming and chancy.*
>
> WARREN BUFFETT

Make sure there hasn't been any significant loss of investment personnel before investing in a managed fund. Key-person risk is high for many top-performing funds. You'd like to think that the success of your investment doesn't ride on the back of one person – or, if it does, that that person will stick around.

Index funds

One of the big debates in investing is whether investment managers should use an active or passive approach. An active investment approach means that the fund managers seek out investments, such as shares, that will do better than the average investment return, or the market. A passive investment approach means an investor does not try to beat the market, rather they accept the market return and try to replicate it through an 'index fund'.

An index is a collection of all the investments in a given category, usually weighted according to their size. It is used to measure the overall performance of all the assets in that category. For example, the index of the largest 200 companies listed on the ASX is known as the ASX 200 index. It measures the average performance of the largest 200 companies by value. Most indices are value weighted, which means larger companies have more importance in the index. In the ASX 200 index, for example, companies such as BHP, the major banks and Telstra have more weight, so changes in their price influence the index more than changes in the prices of smaller companies.

Indices were set up as measuring devices, and the first of them was established by a publisher, Charles Dow, founder of *The Wall Street Journal*. Dow and one of his staff, Eddie Jones, created the Dow Jones Industrial Average, which still exists today as an index made up of thirty of the largest American companies. After a while, research into the investment performance of active fund managers found that very few of them could beat the index over an extended period.

In the early 1970s in the United States, the first 'index fund' was developed by John Bogle, the founder of Vanguard, and he became the great evangelist of index funds. They are a kind of managed fund with a unique style: unlike most managed funds, which are actively managed through the buying and selling of assets, index funds are passively managed. All they do is hold the investments that exist in an index, in the proportion that they appear in that index. The return of an index fund is therefore simply the return on the index, less costs.

'Index funds' are portfolios of investments that match the profile and performance of a given index, such as the ASX 200, the S&P 500 or the NASDAQ. Depending on the nature of the relevant index, these funds can provide a well-diversified portfolio.

The job of an index fund manager is pretty simple – much simpler than an active fund manager, who is looking to consistently beat the index, poring over balance sheets and visiting thousands of companies. All the index fund manager needs to do is make sure the fund continues to match the relevant index, and to achieve the same rate of return as it.

Index funds are therefore a cheap way of investing, because there is little research or trading cost involved in putting together a portfolio that has the same profile of investments as the index. Index funds tend to hold stocks longer than active fund managers, creating fewer transaction costs. They do not have the same level of management costs of actively managed funds. So, if you're happy with the average market return, they're probably the way to go.

Relative performance of index funds

Evidence from the past two decades shows that many managed funds fail to beat the average market return, as measured by the market index. All that active running around, busily trading stocks and trying to beat the market, was for many funds a waste of time.

The average level of relative underperformance has been as high as 3 or 4 per cent over extended periods. Russ Wermers, a professor of finance at the University of Maryland, observed in 2000 that, while fund managers had some ability to select stocks that outperformed the market, the funds still underperformed the index, primarily because of the fees and transaction costs associated with actively managed funds. Even in the presence of investment skill, the inefficiency of managed funds meant the investor ended up with below-average returns. Research by InvestSMART has found that managed funds, on average, underperform their benchmarks by an amount approximately equal to their fees.

This does not mean, however, that index funds are always preferable over actively managed funds. The comparison results are based on averages, but the top-performing managed funds can still outperform the index funds, even if many of the active funds do not. The trick for investors is to find one of the better funds. A good (unconflicted) financial planner should be able to do this for you.

Combining index funds and managed funds

There is a trend towards using a combination of index funds and active funds in portfolios. The index funds provide a diversified, low-cost 'core' to the portfolio, while the use of some active investing adds the prospect of higher performance relative to the index return. The pros and cons of these funds reflect their constituent parts: hybrid funds offer somewhat lower risk and lower transaction costs than actively managed funds, but are unlikely to perform as well as the top managed funds.

Listed funds and trusts

Managed funds are unit trusts that may be listed on the ASX or unlisted, so you can only invest through a prospectus or product disclosure statement. Some unit trusts are listed and traded on the ASX. These include property trusts, exchange-traded funds (ETFs) and listed investment companies. As I discussed in Chapter 8, today's ASX offers access to nearly every category of investment that you might need.

Exchange-traded funds

Index funds and listed exchange-traded funds (ETFs) are similar to each other in that they invest in all the underlying assets of a particular market or index. Where they differ is that traditional index funds have a limited number of units and must be bought and sold via financial planners or the fund manager, whereas ETFs are able to issue new units that can be bought and sold on the stock market, just like shares.

Using the example of an ETF based on the S&P (Standard & Poor's) 500 Index, investors gain exposure to all of the top 500 shares listed on the US market. An Australian investor could use this ETF to 'buy' the US market and diversify internationally without exposing themselves to the risk of losses in single US companies or sectors – just to the market as a whole.

Like ordinary index funds, ETFs passively track the performance of a particular market index, such as the ASX 200. Some ETFs hold all underlying securities in a given index while others select a representative sample.

The most popular ETFs track leading Australian, US, European and Asian share market indices. For example, investors who want exposure to the Chinese market can buy the MSCI China ETF, an index fund that tracks shares in so-called 'red-chip' mainland Chinese companies listed in Hong Kong. Other ETFs track exchange rates, commodities (including gold and silver), and market sectors not well represented on the Australian share market, such as information technology, biotechnology and pharmaceuticals.

The main providers of ETFs in Australia are ANZ, UBS, Vanguard, State Street, VanEck, Russell Investments, BlackRock, BetaShares and Aii (Australian Index Investments).

ETFs are low cost. Like index funds, there is a low turnover of securities within the fund and low management costs because there is less need for extensive company research. The difference in fees between ETFs and managed funds can be significant.

ETFs are good for investors who want to get into the share-market but don't want to pick the companies themselves, and who want low fees. As discussed, fund managers tend to do worse than the market by the amount of their fees. That's definitely true of ETFs – since they just invest in the market and charge a fee – but at least the fee is the lowest you can get.

Listed managed investments and listed investment companies

Listed managed investments and listed investment companies (LICs) are close relatives of managed funds. They are ASX-listed companies carrying on the business of managing an investment portfolio. Effectively, they are managed funds that can be traded on the stock exchange like ordinary shares. Investing in an LIC means that you become part-owner of the underlying investment portfolio. This is what you effectively get when you invest in a managed fund, but the formal legal structure is different.

Even though many LICs are low cost, have good performance histories and closely resemble managed funds, they account for a much smaller portion of the investment landscape. Two of the best-known and best-managed LICs, the Australian Foundation Investment Company and Argo Investments, have been around since 1928 and 1946 respectively.

Once considered dowdy, LICs are back in favour due to their costs, performance, low minimum investment (you can basically invest as little as you like) and liquidity, since you can buy and sell on the market without having to fill out any paperwork. The older LICs are known for the integrity of their management, low fees and reliable returns. They've been joined in recent years by many new funds run by successful fund managers (and some not so successful) striking out on their own.

LICs invest in a portfolio of shares, just like managed funds, but there are important differences. Managed funds are unit trusts where the units are bought and sold through a fund manager, whereas LICs are companies with shares that can be traded on the share market through a broker. This creates important tax differences for investors.

When LICs make profits on the sale of underlying investments, they pay tax on their profits at the company rate and may then pay fully franked dividends to investors. By comparison, managed funds distribute all their profits to investors who then pay tax at their marginal rate.

Units in managed funds are priced according to the total value of the fund's assets divided by the units on issue, but the share price of an LIC is determined by the market. This means the shares can trade at a premium or a discount to their net tangible asset backing, and this sometimes creates the opportunity to buy at prices below the value of their assets.

LICs have low fees, ranging from as little as 0.2 per cent to 1 per cent, compared with average fees of about 2 per cent for retail managed funds. Some of the newer LICs add a performance fee. Investors pay brokerage when they buy or sell, but there are no entry or exit fees.

Investment strategy for managed funds

Some managed funds are more actively managed than others. Some are riskier, and some emphasise particular types of assets, or particular approaches to investing – such as focusing on ethical and low carbon investments. The 'flavour' of any given fund is set out in its prospectus and other documentation such as annual reports. Ratings services like Lipper and Morningstar compare the different funds in particular categories and rate them according to how well they have performed against a given benchmark, such as the relevant market index.

With thousands of different funds on offer, choosing the right one can be a daunting task, but sheer numbers can be deceptive. Most fund managers offer the same pool of assets in different packaging. Take the example of a fund manager who puts together a portfolio of Australian shares marketed as Diversified Australian Equities Fund. This fund is offered in different legal frameworks and at different prices depending on whether you are wealthy or of more modest means, investing inside or outside super, or already drawing a pension.

From your point of view as an investor, managed funds are not designed for short-term trading; they are designed to be held for a minimum of three to five years. Nevertheless, managed funds do offer high liquidity (along with much administrative simplicity). They are easy to enter and exit. It is usually only a matter of days for a managed fund investment to be sold and returned to the investor as cash. Managed funds provide a consolidated tax statement at the end of each year. You can usually follow the performance of the managed fund through the fund manager's website.

Biggest isn't always best

As I mentioned earlier, large investment funds can be victims of their own success. The manager of a large fund might quickly run out of outstanding opportunities. They then have to put money into companies that they see as 'good' and perhaps some into ones they see as merely 'sound'. More 'boutique' funds can focus on smaller companies and higher performing ones.

Two Australian fund management success stories are the Platinum International Fund, which is part of Kerr Neilson's Platinum Asset Management group, and WAM Capital, part of Wilson Asset Management. Kerr Neilson's Platinum International Fund has returned a compound annual return of 12.7 per cent since inception in 1995, and Geoff Wilson's WAM Capital has returned 17.5 per cent per annum since it started in 1999, which is even more impressive.

As noted in the discussion of 'star fundies', with boutique managed funds there is usually 'key-person risk' with respect to the main fund manager. If the fund is led by a particularly talented manager, then the effect of his or her leaving the fund is likely to be significant.

Fees for managed funds

Having a manager look after your investments means that you are accessing the manager's skills and expertise – you're basically hiring someone to manage your money. As in other industries, these skills and expertise come at a cost, and there is a huge range of fees. Some, but not many, charge less than 1 per cent (of your total sum), and others charge as much as 2 to 3 per cent, including performance fees.

The average return from the stock market over the past fifty years has been 8.6 per cent per annum. A fee of 2 per cent is nearly a quarter of that, so obviously you're looking for something better than the average market return, otherwise why pay that kind of fee? On a portfolio of $200,000, 2 per cent is $4000 a year, which is quite a chunk. The fees are paid to the manager out of the fund's capital. Whenever you invest in a managed fund, the question you have to ask is whether the fund will earn returns (at a suitable level of risk) to justify the costs.

One more thing about fees: the cost of them compounds. Take a simple, theoretical example. If you invested $1 million over ten years at an annual rate of return of 10 per cent, the result is $2.59 million. If an annual fee of 1 per cent is taken out, which is $10,000 in year one, the final sum reduces to $2.37 million – that is, the cost of that 1 per cent fee is not ten times $10,000, but more twice that, or $220,000.

This is why I joined InvestSMART as editor-in-chief in 2018 – because they had capped the fees on their ETF investment products. That is, the fees are 0.55 per cent up to $451 and then it stays at that no matter how much money you have in the fund. The effect of that is that the fees don't compound. Because InvestSMART uses ETFs that are provided by others, there is still a small percentage fee – about 0.2 per cent – on top of the $451, but the compounding effect is much less. In the above example, of $1 million over ten years at 10 per cent compound return, a fee of 0.2 per cent plus $451 per year would cost $51,510 over the ten years instead of $220,000 for a 1 per cent fee.

Managed funds and index funds

ETFs have experienced massive growth in Australia and overseas in the past few years – a vote of low confidence in active funds managers. But despite the growing popularity of index funds and ETFs, actively managed funds still make up a large share of managed funds in Australia. You can find share funds that invest in large companies or small companies, industrial companies, high-dividend yield companies or resources stocks. You can also buy funds that specialise in Australian bonds, emerging market debt, Chinese shares, global brands, gold or global listed property.

Actively managed funds generally benchmark their returns against an appropriate index. But rather than investing in each and every security that makes up the index, they invest selectively, based on their research and their investment philosophy.

For example, funds that invest in Australian 'large-cap' shares generally aim to beat the performance of the S&P/ASX 200 Accumulation Index. 'Large-cap' is market shorthand for the top 200 listed companies, ranked by their share market capitalisation, or value. You can work out a company's market value by multiplying the number of shares on issue by the current share price.

Australian small-cap share funds use the S&P/ASX Small Ordinaries Accumulation Index as their benchmark. Global large-cap share funds use the MSCI World Accumulation Index. Australian listed property funds use the S&P/ASX 200 A-REIT Accumulation Index, while Australian fixed-interest funds use the UBS Composite (Fixed Interest) 0+ Years Index, and so forth.

Because index funds aim to replicate the performance of an index, all funds based on the same index ought to hold the same underlying investments and provide the same returns. The only difference ought to be in the management fee charged by the fund manager and hence the index fund's after-tax return.

Index funds charge substantially lower fees than actively managed funds because they do not have to pay for a team of researchers and they trade infrequently. If an index manager is charging substantially more than a manager of a near-identical fund, then you need to ask why. This is one instance where cheapest is generally best.

Pros and cons of exchange-traded funds

I must admit, I'm not a big fan of ETFs and index funds, mainly because you're investing in companies according to size – the bigger they are, the more money you invest in them. I understand that doing so helps you to match the index, but what's so good about that anyway? Against that, I recognise that most active managers don't do better than the market, mainly because they cost more, and the key advantage of ETFs is the low cost.

The problem is that in the Australian market, investing in the index means investing a large proportion of your money in the big four banks and the big miners, BHP and Rio Tinto, simply because they are the biggest companies. But is that a good idea? And after all the revelations out of the banking royal commission, do you really want to invest in those banks?

Maybe you do, but in my view you should make a conscious decision to do so – not just invest in the index and think you're not making a decision, that you're investing 'passively'. In investing, to not make a decision is to make one.

Having said that, I understand why a lot of investors want to have at least part of their portfolio in an index fund: so they don't have to worry about it.

And it's also true that there are a growing number of niche ETFs, which invest in specific sectors or geographies, such as robotics or India. There's no doubt that these are the best way to get some exposure to those things, rather than trying to pick the best companies in those areas yourself. Either go for an index or choose a good specialist managed fund.

Warren Buffett says retail investors should just invest in ETFs, but of course he wouldn't do that himself (not that he's an ordinary retail investor, of course). I hesitate to disagree with the great man but, well, I do. It's your money, I say. Make a decision about it, and don't be passive.

Investors should not just buy whole-market indices: if you want to invest in the big banks, go ahead – but make a decision!

Also, the performance of the whole index is not bad, but it is not great – 8.6 per cent over the long term, as we've already seen. To build significant wealth, you need to do better than that. (If you had bought CSL shares in 1994, you would have achieved a 25 per cent return; so it pays to be strategic and to have good advice.)

Just consider the difference in wealth creation between the average market return of 8.6 per cent and WAM Capital's 17.5 per cent. Saving $672 per month (which is the mandatory super deduction of 9.5 per cent from average weekly earnings) and earning 8.6 per cent over forty years produces a final sum of $1.1 million.

Using Geoff Wilson's 17.5 per cent return instead, the calculator produces a final sum of $8.4 million.

That's the power of compound interest with a higher rate of return. Now it's true that you can't be sure the fund managers you choose can earn that sort of return in future, but it's a fair bet that they can. Why not give at least some of your money to someone who knows what they are doing?

ETFs are also the foundation of a couple of modern investment products that have appeared in the past few years: robo-advice and 'millennial' super funds.

Robo-advice is a sophisticated computer program that asks you some questions and comes up with an asset allocation that supposedly suits you. It's meant to replicate what human advisers do, but of course it can't really do that because it is a machine. Mostly, robo-advice programs are used as 'lead generation' tools for ETF operations. That is, they provide the advice for free and charge when you follow the advice by putting your money into the company's ETF-based funds.

I'm not saying there's anything inherently wrong with this – after all, it's cheap. But then again, you usually get what you pay for.

There are also a few new super funds popping up that are aimed at millennials, that is, people under about thirty-five. Two of them are Spaceship Super and Zuper. Mind you, nearly everyone is under thirty when they start saving in a super fund, because it's mandatory once you start work, but these new ones have a marketing package designed to appeal more to young people making a choice of fund.

To keep costs down, these funds tend to invest most of the money in ETFs, with some extra technology-style investments to generate some excitement. Again, nothing wrong with that at all – in fact, an ETF core with some growth-based strategies on top is a very good, and very common, investment plan.

Tax efficiency and managed funds

Many managed funds are managed with little or no concern for individual investors' tax circumstances. The high level of trading in managed funds can cause tax problems. In a typical fund, as much as 100 per cent of the value of the fund's assets might be traded each year, potentially creating capital gains tax obligations that you must bear. If you are investing in any kind of managed fund, these are the things you need to discuss when seeking advice from your financial planner and your accountant.

Conclusion

To invest, you either DIY or hire someone to help you. Doing it yourself can be a lot of fun, but it's tricky and takes time and focus to get it right. So for most people, hiring someone is the way to go, and most people – everyone who's working, in fact – 'hires' a super fund to look after their savings, even if they don't know it. Investing in a managed fund of some sort is also hiring someone to look after your money, and I hope I've impressed on you that that's the way to approach it: who are they, do you trust them, and, most importantly, what do they charge? You'd ask those questions when engaging an accountant or a plumber, so do it when you're engaging an investment manager. Chances are you'll find someone great!

10

Alternative Asset Classes

I'VE NEVER REALLY LIKED THE TERM 'ALTERNATIVE', although I suppose some word is needed for investments that aren't shares, bonds, property or cash, which is what it basically means. (Some funds even class property as an alternative!) As a group, these are not investments for beginners. But you will hear a lot about them, and your advisers or fund managers might invest in them on your behalf. In many cases, the word 'alternative' simply means 'high fees'. Alternative asset managers, such as hedge funds and private equity funds, have traditionally charged more than anyone else: usually '2 and 20', which means a 2 per cent base fee and a 20 per cent performance fee. The only way they can get away with that is by describing themselves as 'alternative' asset managers who do something different and therefore earn higher returns and deserve higher fees.

It's rubbish. A lot of the time they don't make higher returns, and in any case why should they get higher fees just because their clients take more risk?

Having said that, 'alternative' investments can provide some real diversity by giving investors exposure to assets that aren't correlated to the share market, or the economy, so we should look at what they are and what they do – because, for ordinary investors like you and me, 'alternatives' can actually lower risk. Infrastructure is a case in point.

Infrastructure funds

Infrastructure is often classed as an 'alternative' investment, particularly when a super fund invests in it directly, rather than through an external fund. Infrastructure funds invest in public infrastructure assets such as airports, toll roads, telecommunications installations, ports, rail, and utilities such as powerlines and gas pipelines. These assets are costly to build but they have limited competition and tend to provide a steady income stream over a long period of time. Funds with mature assets may concentrate on providing a steady income stream via dividends or distributions, while funds with newer assets might focus on medium-term capital growth. Infrastructure is a great investment for superannuation because it's long term and low risk, especially if it's something with a monopoly, like a toll road or an airport.

But how do you invest in infrastructure? Well, it's difficult to buy a piece of a significant unlisted asset, like Melbourne airport, but you can buy a piece of Sydney airport because it's listed on the ASX as a company. And of course you can buy shares in Transurban, Australia's largest toll road operator, or gas pipeline operator APA Group, or the electricity 'poles and wires' owner Spark Infrastructure.

Hedge funds

Hedge funds, also referred to as 'absolute return funds', are a gung-ho type of managed fund. The manager of a hedge fund uses active trading strategies to generate investment returns. These strategies can include borrowing money, trading derivatives, short selling (where the fund takes a position that benefits from falls in investment values), program trading and arbitrage trading (looking to trade on price differences of a stock or commodity listed on different exchanges). In short, hedge funds have a broad scope to act as aggressive traders seeking investment returns.

ASIC, in its July 2015 'Snapshot of the Australian Hedge Funds Sector', commented on the growth and diversity of hedge funds, and their occasionally low average returns (only 4.2 per cent in the year to September 2014). Other key trends included the significant participation of retail investors in hedge funds (representing between two-thirds and three-quarters of the investment value), and the funds' emphasis on investments in shares and cash. An earlier bulletin, published by the Reserve Bank, noted that the Australian hedge fund industry had grown much more quickly than either the broader managed fund sector or the global hedge fund industry.

Private equity

'Private equity' used to be called 'leveraged buyouts' but the new name sounds classier and less disreputable. Basically, it means buying whole companies and taking them private (if they are listed), then running them for a while before 'flipping' them, usually after five years or so. The typical PE fund would give the managers of the business powerful financial incentives to cut costs and get the profit up in the short term. And they would increase their own returns by borrowing heavily to make the investment, which is why they were called leveraged buyouts.

Because private equity funds buy and control the underlying businesses, they can borrow against them, and they can make decisions about management and strategic direction. Private equity funds are a bit like the renovators who 'flip' houses. These funds buy businesses, strip out costs, gear up, then 'flip' the businesses.

Sometimes private equity doesn't work; they hit problems with governance or tax, or they simply stuff up the 'flip'. Even when the process does work, the resulting businesses are highly leveraged. For these other reasons, private equity investments are highly risky. Private equity is definitely not for novices or worriers.

Private equity investing is not generally accessible to 'retail' or general investors, and the only way to do it is through a big super fund, which will usually have 5 to 10 per cent of its money in private equity. Big super funds, for example, have been increasing their investment in private equity funds. This has been a key driver of the super funds' higher returns.

Derivatives

Securities such as options, warrants and CFDs derive their prices from underlying assets such as shares, bonds and commodities – they are basically bets on the price of the underlying asset. Because derivatives give exposure to real assets for a relatively low upfront payment, they offer leverage that is like borrowing, which increases risk and magnifies potential gains and losses.

If used well, derivatives have the potential to improve your overall portfolio returns. However, they are notoriously hard to value (and to audit). Due to their complexity and high risk, they are definitely not for novices.

Options

Options are an important variety of derivative security. They come in two types: 'puts' and 'calls'.

Put options give you the right, but not the obligation, to sell a security at a predetermined price in the future. With a put option, you bet that the value of that security will be lower in the future than it is now, so you have sold it at a higher price than the prevailing one in future. Call options, in contrast, give you the right, but not the obligation, to buy a security at a certain price in the future. With a call option, you are betting that the value of the security will be higher in future.

If your bet is wrong and your option is 'out of the money', then you can simply walk away having lost nothing more than your initial outlay in buying the option. As with all derivatives, the pricing and trading of options is complex. More information is available from the ASX website.

You can buy options on individual stocks, share market indices and commodities for a fraction of the upfront price. Options have a specified shelf life. The longer the term, and the more protection you are prepared to pay for, the more expensive the contract price that is set by the market. If you use a put option as insurance against a fall in value in your real share portfolio and the market goes up, not down, then you simply forfeit the cost of your put option and walk away, but you also effectively reduce the profit on your shares.

Contracts for difference (CFDs)

A CFD is a contract between you and a licensed provider that can be traded online. They can be bought on local and international stocks, indices or foreign exchanges for an upfront payment, which is typically 5 to 10 per cent of the value of the shares or 1 per cent for indices. This is what the professionals call leverage – that is, the ability to extract more profit per dollar outlaid. But CFDs also have the potential to magnify losses. For example, if you pay $1000 for $10,000 worth of shares and the share price falls 10 per cent, you will lose your entire outlay. If your losses exceed your initial outlay, you must top up your investment to restore the original loan-to-valuation ratio (LVR).

To reduce potential losses, investors can increase their outlay as a percentage of the underlying equity. Alternatively, they can use a stop loss. For example, if you buy a stock at $10 and set a stop loss at $9.50, your potential loss is limited to half your capital on a 10 per cent LVR.

Unlike options, CFDs have no set expiry date, although in practice most people hold them for weeks rather than months – in other words, they are best left to dedicated traders. One of the main reasons for the quick turnaround is the fact that the interest you pay to the CFD provider is charged daily.

CFDs allow you to bet on the difference between the price of shares today and their price at some specified time in the future. Unlike other derivatives, such as options that hold the same promise, CFDs have a lower upfront cost and are easier to understand because price movements are worked out on a simple one-for-one basis. Hence, if the underlying share price rises by 25 cents, so do your CFDs. Like other derivatives, CFD holders don't own the underlying asset but they do receive dividend payments.

Unless you know what you are doing, CFDs can be hazardous to your wealth. At their best, they can be used to hedge against a sharp fall in your share portfolio. In practice, they are most often used by short-term traders looking to make a quick profit but who are just as likely to incur a big loss.

Alternative investments strategy

A small amount of exposure to hedge funds, private equity or infrastructure in a portfolio can act like insurance. Such alternative assets often have little or no correlation with other asset classes; their prices move independently. In small doses – I would suggest no more than 5 to 10 per cent of your total investment – they have the potential to reduce volatility and smooth overall returns.

The GFC gave a big whack to nearly all asset classes: international property, Australian shares, international shares, commodities, others. But some funds from one category in particular did very well. Hedge funds that 'shorted' America's banks, and the mortgage-backed securities they issue, did spectacularly well. Their performance is dramatised in Michael Lewis's book *The Big Short* and in the film of the same name. (Short selling as a strategy is explored later in this chapter.)

Alternative investments strategy example: Blue Sky

Blue Sky appeared in the Australian market with a name that promised unlimited upside. The promoters of Blue Sky marketed it via financial planners as a way for smaller, retail investors to access the markets for private equity and other 'alternative assets' such as venture capital, hedge funds and infrastructure – the assets such as pension funds and large institutions that were usually only accessible to big funds and high-wealth investors. Big investors typically have a share of their capital allocated to the 'alternative assets' category.

Mark Sowerby set up Blue Sky in 2006. It was a good idea, and I interviewed Mark a few times in the early years. The business grew rapidly and Mark had a large and happy following, eventually giving access to as many as sixty different funds, covering sectors such as water, property, infrastructure and much else besides. The venture made a splash; people piled in, either by buying into the listed entity directly or by investing via fund managers. The idea of giving 'ordinary small investors' access to alterative assets was highly attractive to many people.

But there was a problem at the heart of the Blue Sky model that a lot of us missed. The stock market valued Blue Sky as if it were an alternative assets hedge fund, because that's how it marketed itself. Such funds trade at up to five or six times the value of the underlying assets; this is because hedge funds can often achieve spectacular growth (and often take spectacular risks).

In reality, though, around half of Blue Sky's assets were actually just plain old commercial property. So Blue Sky was half a REIT, and, as I mentioned in the previous chapter, REITs were trading at just 1 to 1.2 times assets. Blue Sky resembled a REIT in another way, too: it charged investors fees against the whole of its assets, including those funded by borrowings. That might be okay for REITs, which charge low-ish fees, but Blue Sky wasn't charging REIT-level fees. It was charging like a hedge fund. There was a chasm at the heart of the model.

At this point, an American hedge fund, Glaucus Research, entered the picture. Glaucus has a simple business model. It looks for houses of cards, and it blows them over. It does this by 'short selling' investments, and then publishing highly adverse research reports in very negative language. Short selling involves borrowing shares from someone who owns them, usually a big super fund, and then selling them – going into a negative ownership position, by selling an asset that the short seller has borrowed and does not own. You can also do it with contracts for difference, or CFDs, by betting that the price will fall. This sounds a bit like black magic, but it isn't really. It's just making a bet that a price will fall. With Glaucus, they just make it a bit more certain by giving it a shove.

Glaucus's sixty-page report on Blue Sky was as damning as it was sensational. For example:

Blue Sky Gouges Australian Investors with Extortionate Fees. Because of fee pressure on asset managers in recent years, only the world's best can charge some variation of 2/20: a 2 per cent management fee and a 20 per cent performance fee. Yet, hidden in the fine print of Blue Sky's investment documents, we discovered that Blue Sky consistently charged Australian investors extortionate management fees as high as 17 per cent. These are not performance fees tied to the success of the investments. Rather, Blue Sky charges such fees up front and labels them as management fees, establishment fees, due diligence fees or other advisory fees. Not only are Blue Sky's ludicrous upfront fees an abusive practice that gouges the very investors Blue Sky claims to serve, but Blue Sky's revenues will continue to shrink as it runs out of suckers to pay such exorbitant fees.

This was Glaucus's second venture of this type in Australia. The short seller's first target, Quintis, saw its share price fall 77 per cent after the publication of the Glaucus report, and eventually the company went broke. That rather increased Glaucus's credibility, which hugely increased the impact of its work on Blue Sky. The short selling method was a powerful weapon.

Glaucus's Blue Sky report raised multiple concerns, including with the fund manager's approach to valuing its assets. Blue Sky was a new venture with few benchmarks, especially for smaller investors. They had to rely on audited valuations and reports – but as we all know, auditors often get it wrong. Blue Sky's share price fell from around $11 to $1.95. It is now trading at a REIT multiple of around 1 times its assets. A value of around 1 times is another way of saying Blue Sky is adding zero value to the underlying property portfolio (known as net tangible assets). It is also a way of saying that the business is being valued as if it were in distress.

Hedge funds strategy

Just because something is called a hedge fund doesn't necessarily mean it's risky. For example, some hedge funds actually live up to their name and 'hedge' their risk by using derivatives to take out insurance against big losses.

Hedge funds, like all 'alternatives', are usually promoted to investors as having a low correlation with traditional asset classes, and the ability to make money from trading strategies in either rising or falling markets. Low correlation means that the returns received are not closely related; they don't tend to move together. This is useful in an overall portfolio because hedge funds and other alternatives may provide a higher investment return at a time when other investment returns are poor, thus evening out the overall return.

✓ **Tip:** Ask yourself: Do you feel well informed about the investment product? Can you describe in simple terms how it actually works? If you don't understand the product, don't invest in it.

There aren't many retail hedge funds around – they're mostly wholesale funds offered to large super funds to 'juice up' their returns. Mostly they wouldn't invest more than about 5 per cent of their portfolio in hedge funds, which I think is a pretty good limit.

Numerous hedge funds aim to make a positive return each and every year; this is why they are often referred to as 'absolute return funds'. In reality, however, few funds achieve this ambitious aim.

Because hedge funds aim to be uncorrelated to the market, their performance depends of the skill of their managers. No matter how sophisticated their algorithms and trading systems, people are fallible. There have been some spectacular hedge funds failures since the sector began to take off in the 1990s. One example is the fall of Long-Term Capital Management in 1998.

LONG-TERM CAPITAL MANAGEMENT

Long-Term Capital Management (LTCM) was a large hedge fund led by Nobel Prize–winning economists (Myron Scholes and Robert Merton) and renowned Wall Street traders. Due to LTCM's high-risk trading strategies, it almost collapsed in 1998.

The fund started with just over $1 billion in initial assets. At the fund's height in 1998, it had approximately $5 billion in assets, but, thanks to leverage, it controlled over $100 billion, and had positions with a total value of over $1 trillion. At the time, LTCM had borrowed assets worth more than $120 billion.

Due to this very high leverage, along with a bond default in Russia, LTCM sustained large losses and was in danger of its own default. In September 1998, the fund ('too big to fail') was bailed out with the help of the US Federal Reserve. A crisis was narrowly averted, but it set a dangerous precedent for future market conduct and future bailouts.

Private equity strategy

Let's return briefly to the field of 'private equity' and consider it from the point of view of investment strategy.

Private equity basically means a fund that buys whole companies instead of just investing in shares. The advantage of that is they get to decide what happens and can cut costs and increase debt – both of which they usually do with abandon!

The disadvantage is that whole companies are hard to sell – you can't just put an offer on the ASX and watch it get taken up by buyers. Often private equity funds float their companies on the ASX once they are finished with them, and because that's such a big deal, they don't do it very often. The typical holding period for a private equity investment is five to seven years.

There are a growing number of private equity managed funds available for investors. These managed funds often have high minimum investment balances and are relatively 'illiquid' – that is, it may take a very long time for an investor to be able to sell their investment, if they can at all. As an example, Gresham is a private equity firm that has managed successful private equity funds for investors. In 2004, it established Gresham Private Equity Fund 2, which required a minimum investment of $50,000, although this amount was not all paid at the start of the investment, but in instalments as required. Since its establishment, the fund has made a number of purchases, including Pacific Print Group and Witchery Fashions. It is likely to be five or ten years before investors receive returns from their investment.

Private equity funds listed on the ASX include the Cordish Dixon Private Equity Funds, ING Private Equity Access Limited and Macquarie Global Private Equity Securities Fund. Because these funds are listed, it is possible to buy and sell them more easily. Private equity funds have a reputation for charging high fees. As always, it is crucial that you understand the level of fees you are paying and that you are comfortable with these before you decide to invest.

Short selling

Most investors buy shares they hope will go up in price – in other words, they buy low to sell high. That's called investing 'long'. 'Short selling', which is mostly done by hedge funds, is the reverse: you're betting that something will fall in price, by selling high with the aim of buying low later. Short selling, in short, is the practice of borrowing shares to sell on the market with a view to buying them back at a lower price in the near future and repaying your 'loan' with cheaper shares.

Investors do this because they think a stock is overvalued or is about to be the subject of a negative announcement, and hence likely to go down. Or investors may wish to protect their portfolio against a general market fall by shorting a number of stocks or a market index. Used in this way, short selling acts as a kind of insurance and is commonly employed by hedge funds and absolute return funds to manage risk.

This is how it's done. You think Acme Industries is headed for a price fall. You short 1000 shares trading at $10 a share, their current trading price. You borrow those shares from your broker, who sells them at the going price and deposits the $10,000 from the sale in your account. At the end of the investment period, you have to close out the loan. Assume the share price has fallen to $5. You buy 1000 shares in the market for $5000 and return the shares to your broker. That leaves you with a profit of $5000, excluding brokerage. If you bought back at a higher price, say, $15, you would still return the shares to your broker, but you would have lost $5000.

The big risk with short selling is that the loss can be infinite, whereas when you're investing 'long', you can only lose what you've invested. That is, if you get it wrong, and the stock you have shorted goes up instead of down, there's no theoretical limit to how far it can go up. On the way down, on the other hand, it can't go past zero.

Only certain securities are approved for short selling on the ASX, mostly larger, liquid stocks. The ASX applies other rules, too, for short selling, including how quickly short positions need to be settled, and requirements to maintain margin cover for big price movements. Check with the ASX or your broker about this. Frequently shorted shares in Australia include Domino's, Myer and JB Hi-Fi.

THE FIRST SHORT SELLER

The world's first short seller was an Australian. Born in Melbourne in 1901, Alfred Winslow Jones moved to the United States. He became interested in managing money while working for *Fortune* magazine in 1949 and raised US$100,000 (a good chunk of money at that time) to set up a partnership and develop the first hedge fund.

Direct investment in businesses

Buying into a business directly is sometimes an option for investors. You might be invited to buy a franchise or to invest directly in a small or medium-sized business. In all such cases, you need to be on your guard. I've seen hundreds of cases where people have been burnt, often by things in the fine print, or by hazards they never expected. Here are some sound questions to ask.

QUESTIONS TO ASK WHEN INVESTING IN A BUSINESS

- Is the business consistently generating strong cashflows?
- Does it own significant physical assets such as land and equipment?
- Does the business have a strong record of paying off debt?
- Do the principal people in the business have good reputations, impeccable integrity and 'skin in the game'?
- Is the business creating intellectual property (such as brands, inventions and creative content) that can be sold or scaled up?
- What industry is it in, and is that industry performing well? (Now may not be the best time, for example, to invest in 'bricks-and-mortar' retail businesses or carbon-intensive sectors.)

Key points about alternative assets

Investing in alternatives can seem pretty complicated and daunting, but the truth is that for most ordinary investors the only one that's directly relevant is infrastructure. That's because industry super funds all have a substantial allocation to it, and because it's accessible to small investors as well – through the ASX.

I'm talking there about stocks like Transurban (toll roads), Sydney Airport, Spark Infrastructure (electricity distribution) and APA Group (gas pipelines). There's not many infrastructure stocks on the ASX, but enough to provide some exposure. There are listed investment companies that specialise in various alternative investments, which can be seen on the ASX website.

Big super funds and professional investors see alternative assets as diversification – you know, a bit of this and a bit of that. Don't put all your eggs in one basket, and all that. You should too. The only problem with doing it through the ASX by buying Transurban and Sydney Airport is that they are still listed companies, and when the ASX goes for a dive, they do too. When super funds invest in infrastructure and other alternatives, they do it 'unlisted', so they're diversifying away from the ASX as well.

Never mind, we can only do what we can do, and as long as you approach those listed infrastructure investments as if they were unlisted – that is, don't check their prices every day, and don't panic if there's a general stock market downturn – you should be fine. Infrastructure assets are fantastic things to invest in, but they are really long term, just like the things they own.

11

Superannuation

REGARDLESS OF WHETHER YOU HAVE ANY OTHER money to invest, everyone should know how to make the most of their super.

My own experience with superannuation is like that of many people in Australia, especially of my age (late sixties), who started working well before compulsory super got going in the early 1990s. For much of my career, I was a wage and salary earner before the era of compulsory super. I moved from job to job pouring all spare cash into ever-expanding mortgages, without paying much attention to saving for retirement. After 1993, I had a bit of super, spread across a few funds. (A system with one big default fund, based on the Future Fund, would have been ideal for me!)

I turned fifty in 2002 and realised I had virtually no superannuation. Holy moly! I had to do something. So I started a business that, I hoped, would create value over and above my salary, and would become the basis for a retirement nest egg. What sort of business? Well, two things guided that decision: writing and otherwise communicating was the only I was good at, and there was a real need to help people escape the clutches of what I saw as a corrupt financial advice and investment system.

I was working for Fairfax and the ABC at the time, and thought Fairfax was more likely than the ABC to want to join me in a commercial investment newsletter, so I wasted six months negotiating with the powers that be in the company, but they couldn't get their heads around partnering with one of their journalists, even if I was a contractor at the time, rather than an employee.

Anyway, in frustration I approached an investment banker friend for financial support, and Eureka Report was born. It succeeded because there was a real appetite for independent analysis, but I couldn't just be satisfied with that, could I? We had to take on the *Financial Review* with *Business Spectator*, which soaked up all of Eureka Report's profits for five years, and then some (which, for me, was borrowed).

I was lucky of course: not everyone has a rich friend who can help them start a business. Most people who wake up at the age of fifty with not enough in super have to think about taking more risks with the super they've got to get the return up, or buy an investment property using the equity in their house and borrowed money. That's risky too.

Not that my business was without risk, but it was a lot of fun, and we got the money back and more when we sold the business to News Corporation in 2012. I had a four-year employment contract with News to serve out, and at the end of that I was sixty-four – a nice time to retire, you might think. Yeah, nah, as the footballers say. I still had work to do.

Apart from the fact that I enjoyed working – writing columns and doing my little spot on the ABC News – I had made the mistake of investing a lot of the proceeds of the sale in a few unlisted start-ups that were meant to have been four- and five-year bonanzas, but which turned out to be six-year struggles, still struggling. They'll get there, I reckon, but so far my only return on them has been an intangible one: the lesson that you're never too old to learn something. And I learned about the benefits of diversification and liquidity, that investing in start-ups can be a lot of fun, and can sometimes be enormously profitable, but you can't get your money out when you need it.

Not that I'm crying poor: I also built a nice portfolio of listed stocks and a couple of investment properties far enough ahead of the end of the boom that they have done well. But as I said, you're never too old to learn.

Liquidity is an important lesson for investors, and like all lessons it's best not to learn it the hard way. Ask yourself, where are the exits? Could you get your money out if you needed to? Is there a liquid market for the investment product? What fees and other costs might apply if you exited early?

All the start-ups that I invested in are run by terrific people, and this was crucial to my investment decision, but good people don't make liquidity when you need it.

The cost of liquidity

While liquidity is important, a lot of the time you don't really need it, and it carries a hidden cost. You can see it in the superior performance of super fund Hostplus, which has produced the top ten-year return of 12.5 per cent thanks largely to having a large proportion of its investments in unlisted, illiquid infrastructure, private equity and venture capital. Other super funds, which have their money in more liquid investments, have produced lower performance.

Super is an inherently illiquid investment – you're simply not allowed to get your money out until you retire, at the right age. I think it's pretty crazy that a lot of super is invested in highly liquid assets – even cash – at low rates of return, even though the money has to stay there for decades. Investment property is also illiquid because it's a big lump and can be hard to sell, and when you do sell there are very high transaction costs, so you don't want to do it too often.

But if you do find, at age fifty, that your retirement sum is looking light on, then trading off liquidity is one way to get your return up. After all, you probably still have another fifteen years. You could, in theory, invest in a fifteen-year term deposit and know for sure what you were going to get at the end. Or you could invest in a start-up that will take fifteen years to mature – in which case you wouldn't have a clue what you'll get at the end, including nothing!

The only truly, reliably, totally liquid investment is an at-call bank account, which is another clear demonstration of the cost of liquidity: the 'overnight cash rate' set by the Reserve Bank is just 1.5 per cent and the banks variously pay only slightly more than that for 'at call' deposits. The only way to get higher interest rates safely is to lock up your money – that is, to trade away liquidity.

To some extent, diversification is about the balance between liquid and illiquid investments, and that balance is purely personal and specifically to do with how old you are. As I've already said, if you're young and saving for retirement, then liquidity is not important – but as you get older and move into retirement, you need more of your money in liquid investments, so you can access it, and live off it.

By the way, diversification is about many other things as well and boils down to the old but true cliché: 'don't put all your eggs into one basket'. That means any basket. Don't invest all your money in Australia just because you live here; don't put too much into the banks, even though they pay a good dividend; don't give all of your money to one fund manager, or even one financial adviser, because they're only human, and humans sometimes make mistakes.

My experience with start-ups also taught me a lesson about diversification, one I already knew in theory. I put too much of my capital into illiquid investments. Some types of investors can tolerate having their capital locked up for a long time. But for ordinary investors, and especially those who, like me, are approaching retirement, a better asset allocation might have seen me put 10 to 20 per cent into high-growth start-ups, but no more than that. For any investor, locking up too much money in illiquid investments means you can't get your cash when you need it.

This is one reason why the 'Buffett Way' is not for everyone. Not all of us can tie up our wealth in long-term positions. Things come up – things that require cash. Health problems, family milestones, irresistible opportunities. Younger and midlife investors who are earning a salary or another type of regular income may be able to afford to leave their investments alone, and to reinvest all the dividends. Retirees, however, typically need to use at least some of the dividends and interest to pay everyday living costs.

There is another way, too, in which the 'Buffett Way' is not for everyone. All Warren Buffett does is invest. He is a professional wealth manager and wealth builder. He is a specialist, with exceptional skills, and for him it's a full-time job. Not everyone can do what he does. Far from it. And few people have the time (or the potential upside) to devote every day to watching markets and analysing companies and economies. Nevertheless, we can still learn a lot from Buffett's approach, and we can apply those lessons when we engage financial advisers and fund managers to do the legwork for us.

HOSTPLUS

Hostplus is a good example of the cost of too much liquidity, and how trading it away can lead to better returns. CEO David Elia explained to me how Hostplus has been the best performing super fund for ten years:

'We have about 13 per cent of our total funds under management invested in direct property, this is unlisted property. We have about 12 per cent invested in infrastructure. We have 7 per cent invested in private equity, 7 per cent allocated to credit, and 8 per cent allocated to what we term as alternatives and that would largely incorporate hedge fund style strategies. All up, we have about 40 per cent invested in the unlisted sector and maybe just to complete the discussion around our asset allocation we have 23 per cent of our funds invested in Australian equities, 22 per cent in international developed market equities, and we have an allocation of 8 per cent to international emerging markets.

'Certainly by virtue of taking that long-term view we have been able to invest in infrastructure types of assets. To simplify it, we are talking about investments in real assets: airports, toll roads and energy infrastructure. An example is our ownership of 50 per cent of the new Sydney entertainment and international convention and exhibition centre, that is a $1.5 billion project … and a PPP-style investment in association with the New South Wales state government.

'Liquidity costs money. One of the things I often like to talk about is risk-adjusted returns. People will talk about the returns that they're generating from listed markets, and more often than not they may seek to benchmark those types of returns to the returns that are generated from unlisted property or infrastructure, but there is very little discussion around the underlying level of risk that is then built into taking those types of positions. Thinking about the types of returns that each of the asset classes are delivering on the risk-adjusted basis, the types of returns that we see delivered from our unlisted portfolio certainly is a much lower level of volatility therefore risk, that you're seeing embedded in those types of investments.

'Enormous amount of volatility are associated with listed equities, and we're certainly seeing that play out now given where markets are at, and markets certainly for this quarter have been in negative territory. Liquidity does come at a price but it depends on which way you want to look at it. The illiquidity premium that some commentators like to talk about in relation to unlisted assets, we certainly see that, we see that both in the context of the absolute return that's generated but also in reduction in the volatility that recently emendated from those types of investments.'

Part of the reason to pay attention to David Elia, apart from the fact that he knows how to invest, is that his methods are likely to spread – for the simple reason that he's successful. Hostplus is influential, and rightly so.

TOP-PERFORMING SUPER FUNDS

In the 2019 Chant West Super Fund Awards, Unisuper was the Fund of the Year. Other winners included:

- Pension fund of the year: Q Super
- Corporate solutions fund of the year: Sunsuper
- Best fund, investments: UniSuper
- Best fund, member services: Sunsuper
- Specialist fund of the year: Hesta
- Best fund, insurance: NGS Super
- Best fund, integrity: First State and VicSuper
- Best fund, innovation: Guild Super
- Best fund, longevity product: Colonial First State

Chant West's head of research, Ian Fryer, said: 'This industry and we as individuals will only succeed if we fulfil our mandate to do what is best for members and to direct all our energies to that goal.'

Sunsuper – who won the award for best fund for member services – had ticked all the boxes for its members. 'It's a strong all-round fund,' he said. 'Sunsuper spends much of its energy in investments on unlisted assets as it believes this is where it can create most value for members. It has a sophisticated program of investments in private equity, property and infrastructure. Performance over the last five years has been strong – consistently top quartile. And its use of member data to identify and promote each member's next best action consistently across multiple channels is more developed than any other fund. Its big investment in this area has yielded impressive results in terms of engagement and members taking positive action. All its campaigns are now automated, which has meant that it can focus its energies on producing engaging content for each communication.'

Super is not an investment

The first thing to keep in mind about super is that it's not an investment, it's a way to invest. More specifically, it's simply a tax-effective structure for investing.

A lot of people ask questions like: 'Are shares a better investment than super?' Or more commonly: 'Is property better than super?' But a better question would be: 'Is it better to own shares or property inside super, or outside?' Superannuation is an investment vehicle – it doesn't compete with shares or property, although it is valid to ask whether it's better to put extra money in a super fund (if you can) or to invest in property outside super and negatively gear.

So super is just a tax structure, a bucket for your savings that is taxed at a lower rate (15 per cent) than the rest of your income when you put it in, and the income on it is also taxed at the same lower rate once it's in the bucket. A whole industry – or, rather, several industries – have developed around the tax structure known as super, designed to help you get access to the tax break in a way that suits you. This chapter is about how you can make the most of it.

The first 'super strategy' question is:

How much should I put into super?

Answer: as much as you can. First, genuine, legitimate tax breaks are hard to come by these days, so you might as well use the ones that are laid out in front of you, with the government and the tax office saying: 'Here, please pay less tax.' Second, a key theme of this book is the importance of harnessing the power of compound interest, and the biggest enemy of that is tax. The simplest and most obvious way to lift your long-term investment return, and therefore the impact of compounding, is to use the superannuation tax break.

In 2017, to save money, the government reduced the amount you can contribute into super, both with and without a tax break. The concessional contributions cap – that is, the amount that can be put in after only 15 per cent tax has been paid on the money – was cut to $25,000 a year. The non-concessional contributions cap was also reduced from $180,000 to $100,000. That's the amount of extra money you can put into the super bucket after your full marginal income tax has been paid on it. Is that still worth doing? Well, yes, because it's only taxed at 15 per cent once it's in there, although, as with all super, you can't get it out until you retire, unless you pay the full tax.

ASIC's MoneySmart website has a free calculator to help you work out how much extra you can and should put into super – it's called the 'Super Contributions Optimiser'. In general, it's usually best to put in the most you can within the cap, and if you earn less than $263,000 per year, you'll have some room to do so, because that's the salary at which the 9.5 per cent compulsory super deduction hits $25,000. Of course, many people earn much less than $263,000 and have a family and a mortgage – so there may be very little spare cash to set aside!

As for the non-concessional cap, that's really about getting a windfall. If a beloved aunt dies and leaves you some money, by all means take a trip or buy a car, but if there's anything left, put it into super. And if you're paid well enough that even after all expenses there's still enough cash left over after putting in the maximum $25,000 concessional contributions, you should definitely put in some more after-tax money as well. As I say: tax breaks are hard to come by.

Switching super funds

If you're not satisfied with your current super fund, you don't have to go all the way to a self-managed superfund – you can just switch funds.

In 2013, the Australian Prudential Regulation Authority (APRA) made it faster to 'roll over' your money from one fund to another by reducing the time that a fund is required to action such requests from thirty to three business days. You just have to fill in something called the 'portability form' on the ATO website, either on paper or online.

There are two sides to that three-day requirement, in my view: it gives members more control over their money, but it also means super funds have to carry a lot of liquid investments, just in case they get a 'run' – that is, where a lot of members want to transfer out at once. As I've been pointing out, liquidity can cost returns, especially when the money is sitting in cash these days, with interest rates where they are. APRA data for the year to June 2018 shows that the average allocation to cash and fixed interest investments in Australian super funds was 30 per cent, or close to a trillion dollars, which means returns are lower than they perhaps should be.

Anyway, there are several reasons why you may decide to switch superannuation funds. You may be starting a new job, or looking to consolidate your superannuation that's sitting in a few accounts. You may be dissatisfied with your existing superannuation fund and want to find an alternative.

To make this decision, you need to understand how and why an alternative superannuation fund would be better than your current fund. You should look at fees, investment performance, insurance coverage and any other services the fund offers.

Also, your current fund may have hidden features. For example, your employer may contribute more to your superannuation fund than the compulsory amount, so you should find out from your employer whether there are other benefits around your superannuation that are related to how long you stay with the company or, indeed, if your money only becomes yours after you have been with the company for a certain period of time – that is, if there's a qualifying period for the extra super contributions.

Performance of superannuation funds is affected not only by the performance of investment markets but also by the fee structure.

When looking at a fund's performance, it is important to look at the investment results over the long term. Superannuation is a long-term proposition: you are not looking to change your super fund every week or month, or even every decade.

Look at the fund's average returns over the past five to ten years. That time frame should allow any bumps in the shorter-term performance results to be averaged away. Otherwise the bumps can exaggerate the very good or very poor performance of a particular fund. The APRA website has a lot of information about super funds, but it's a bit hard to navigate, and there's also an outfit called Superratings, which will give you super fund ratings for free in return for your email address.

Ensure you compare like with like. If you are looking at the performance of your growth-style investment – that is, one that is more heavily weighted towards shares and property – compare it with other growth-style investment options.

Consider the impact that fees have on the fund's performance over the long term. ASIC has estimated that if you pay an extra 1 per cent each year in fees over a thirty-year period, you could reduce your final retirement benefit by up to 20 per cent.

Super fees

Small differences in fees can have a big impact on returns over your investing life. The amount of money available to you in retirement will depend on returns less tax and fees, so fees are an important consideration, although they are not the only one. Let's look again at the impact of fees, with a focus on super.

Super funds charge fees as a percentage of funds under management. So if you have a balance of $100,000 in your super fund and fees of 2 per cent, then you're paying $2000 a year in fees. Now imagine you earn a 5 per cent return on your investment – that 2 per cent fee is eating 40 per cent of your after-tax annual return. Worse still, if your fund loses money, you still pay that 2 per cent fee.

But perhaps the most important thing to understand with fees is that they compound, like investment returns. Take the simple example above: if you invested $100,000 for twenty years at a compound return of 5 per cent, you would end up with $265,379. But if a fee of 2 per cent per annum was taken out, so the net return was 3 per cent, the final sum after twenty years would be only $180,611. That's a difference of $84,718 – more than double the simple calculation of twenty years of $2000. So that's how the magic of compounding works against you with fees.

When you compare fees, you need to ask what you are paying for. Superior performance, personalised financial advice and a high level of service all come at a cost. If your fund charges higher than average fees, then you should expect above-average performance and service, but that is not always the case.

Since the introduction of super choice, fees have been central to the marketing of many superannuation funds, particularly industry superannuation funds, which argue they have not only lower average fees but superior performance as well.

Both of those things are true. According to APRA data, the total operating and administrative expenses of funds with more than four members in 2017–18 was $1.7 billion, or 0.29 per cent of total funds. The equivalent figures for retail funds were $4.2 billion and 0.69 per cent. Industry funds, on average, produced a net return of 9.8 per cent for the year; retail funds produced 7.4 per cent. That difference, over a lifetime (forty years), produces a difference in outcome of exactly double – that is, saving every month for forty years at a return of 9.8 per cent produces a retirement sum of twice the amount that a return of 7.4 per cent would produce.

That difference doesn't just exist over one year either. APRA doesn't publish longer-term results, but industry analysts such as Chant West do. Its results for the year to June 2018 show that industry funds beat retail funds over three, five, seven, ten and fifteen years, by a significant margin. The difference over fifteen years, which is perhaps the most relevant for long-term superannuation, is 8.2 per cent versus 7.1 per cent. For someone saving $673 per month (9.5 per cent of average weekly earnings) for forty years, that makes a difference in retirement of $500,000.

Superannuation and insurance

Insurance coverage is an important differentiator of superannuation funds and products, and can be a real trap. Don't assume coverage is standard in all superannuation funds or that the cost of it is the same. In some cases, it will be compulsory, but in other funds you may have to qualify. Age restrictions may also apply.

While medical examinations may not be compulsory, automatic cover is not necessarily a good thing if it is either not enough cover or too much. Insurance coverage offered by superannuation funds commonly extends to life and disability cover, but does not usually include other forms of insurance, such as income protection.

There can also be huge variations in premiums across super-annuation funds. Research has found that someone could pay twenty-two times more for the same cover at another superannuation fund than the one they're in.

Insurance premiums can have a significant impact on your retirement age and final benefit, so it is important not only to get the right insurance coverage but also to make sure you don't pay too much for it.

Why is there a price differential between premiums? Different types of superannuation funds take into consideration different factors when pricing their premiums. For example, the Chant West research found that industry funds generally base the level of cover and premiums on age only, so there is a high degree of cross-subsidisation within these funds.

Life insurance is an emotive issue. For young parents, it is very easy for a financial planner to encourage them to take out more than they think is necessary, on the grounds that a higher level of cover would mean a better quality of life for the children if both parents should die. This is emotional territory. Just keep in mind that the salesperson is not only driven by a civic-minded desire to see your children thrive in the event of your premature demise.

Life insurance and income-protection insurance are both very expensive and taking it out is a decision to be made carefully and thoughtfully – it shouldn't be something you just a tick a box about, as part of your super. In my view, whether you need it or not is a question of who depends on you being alive and earning money, and how difficult life will be for them if you're not around.

It's a practical purchase that should be approached practically: how big is the mortgage, could your family service it if you died or couldn't work, are there other costs that need to be provided for? Discuss it with your family, and work out a figure, bearing in mind that you have to give up some things to pay the premiums, for safety later.

Topping up your super

As already noted, the maximum amount you can put into super each year at the concessional tax rate of 15 per cent is $25,000. That's 9.5 per cent of $263,158, so if you're earning less than that, you can contribute more to your fund than your employer is taking in compulsory deductions. For example, if you're on a salary of $120,000, you could contribute another $1133 per month, which would make a big difference to your retirement outcome – although of course it would also make a big difference to your monthly spending money, not to mention what's available for paying off the mortgage, so it may not be affordable. But if you can afford a bit of extra saving that you're prepared to lock up till you retire (rather than saving for a holiday), then it's definitely a good idea.

For people who earn less than $28,000 a year, the federal government is currently offering a co-contribution scheme whereby it pays $1.50 for every additional dollar you contribute to your own superannuation (up to a maximum of $1500). Co-contributions are also available for people earning between $28,000 and $58,000 a year. It is adjusted depending on your income and how much you voluntarily contribute to your super fund. This scheme tapers off as income increases up to $58,000. Some conditions apply, so it is worth familiarising yourself with the options. For more information, visit www.asfa.asn.au.

Another thing worth looking at is salary sacrificing. This effectively gives your employer the authority to pay some pre-tax funds from your salary directly to your super fund, over and above the compulsory superannuation rate. As the funds are coming out of your salary before you pay tax, you end up paying less income tax, and because you don't see the funds first, you are not relying on your own discipline to invest the funds when you remember. This approach can be a great option if you want to – and have the capacity to – add a little extra to your super.

In some households with two working-age spouses, one spouse may earn very little super, so it can be a tax-effective strategy to make spouse contributions and reduce the total tax bill for the family. There are limits set on how much can be contributed in a spouse's name. If your spouse earns less than $10,800 a year, you can also make an undeducted or after-tax contribution of $3000 to their super account. This strategy will earn you a tax rebate of $540, one that you can claim every year.

The key message about super is that it's not a tax – it's your money. Think of it as your moneybox. You can, and should, take control of it.

Should you have an SMSF?

One of the great deceptions in super is the idea that self-managed super funds are actually self-managed. A few are, but the vast majority are managed by advisers. In fact, there is a huge industry built around managing SMSFs for people who have opted out of the institutional super fund industry. And the terrible reality is that a lot of those people are persuaded by self-interested advisers to set up their own super fund when they shouldn't, and end up significantly worse off, mainly because of very high fees, charged for not very much.

In June 2018, the Australian Securities and Investments Commission (ASIC) published the results of a study into SMSFs, including an independent review of 250 client files, where someone was advised to set up an SMSF by an adviser who then ran the fund. They found that with 10 per cent of the files the clients risked being 'significantly worse off in retirement as a result of following that advice'.

> Our concerns were based on the balance size of the SMSF, the age of members, and the level of gearing within the fund – or a combination of these factors. ... In a further 47 files (19 per cent), we considered that clients were at increased risk of suffering financial detriment as a result of following the advice. Our concerns were based on the fact that the assets of the fund were to be invested in a single asset class (i.e. property), which appeared to pose an unnecessary risk due to the lack of diversification.

And shockingly, the study found that in 62 per cent of the files – nearly two-thirds – the adviser 'did not demonstrate compliance with the best interests duty and related obligations'.

Separately, ASIC also did an online survey of SMSF trustees (that is, those who were managing the fund on behalf of the family) and found that about a third didn't understand their legal obligations as an SMSF trustee – things like the need for an investment strategy, keeping comprehensive records and getting an annual audit.

A lot of people deal with all this by getting an SMSF adviser to manage the whole thing, which means it's not really 'self-managed' and costs really mount up and, as the other ASIC study showed, there's a 62 per cent chance of getting a bad adviser. Not only are there auditing, accounting and lodgement costs, but also advisers tend to take around 1 per cent (some less, some more) from the account each year to do the investing, so you're no better off than being in a large super fund.

The vast majority of SMSFs are managed by financial advisers and the SMSF structure is just a handy tax vehicle for the investments. But a lot of people do actually manage their own money, either because they're good at it or they enjoy it and want control. The reason you need quite a lot of money to make it worthwhile is that a lot of the costs are in dollars instead of percentages, specifically the accountant and the auditor, who might charge around $2000 a year, all up. If you only had $10,000, for example, that would be 20 per cent, so obviously not worthwhile, since a super fund will charge around 1 per cent, but if you had a million dollars, then an SMSF is cost-effective because it's only 0.2 per cent – less than any super fund.

THE JAMES CRIBB CASE

In July 2018, Queensland financial planner James Cribb was banned from providing advice for four years. After selecting him at random for an investigation, ASIC found that Cribb failed to act in his clients' best interests when providing advice about SMSFs. Cribb owned an SMSF administration business, Mode SMSF, and the advice he gave was likely to benefit that business.

ASIC reviewed a large sample of Cribb's files and found that most did not adhere to the 'best interests' test and other rules. Even worse, in around one in ten files, the advice was likely to leave clients significantly worse off in retirement. Apart from the identified conflict of interest, there were problems with the level of diversification recommended and the level of investment risk.

Trustees of SMSFs must:

- keep accurate and accessible accounting records that explain the transactions and financial position of the fund for a minimum of five years
- prepare an annual operating statement and an annual statement of the fund's financial position and keep these records for a minimum of five years
- prepare minutes of trustee meetings (where matters affecting the fund were discussed), and prepare records of all changes of trustees and members' written consent to be appointed as trustees. Each of these documents must be kept for a minimum of ten years
- keep copies of all annual returns lodged for a minimum of five years
- keep copies of all reports given to members for a minimum of ten years.

(Of course, you don't necessarily have to do all this stuff yourself. Most people just get their accountant to do it, but that's one part of how the costs of running an SMSF mount up.)

INAPPROPRIATE ADVICE: GEARING AND SMSF

The financial planner recommended that James and Carmel establish a series of investments, funded with borrowing, along with a self-managed super fund (SMSF).

As market conditions worsened, the investments were frozen. The financial planner recommended that James and Carmel sell the frozen investments to the SMSF so they could use the proceeds to repay the loans. James and Carmel were left with an investment loss.

They complained that the financial planner's advice was not appropriate as it exposed them to unnecessary risk. The planner's licensee responded that the advice was appropriate as it would enable James and Carmel to achieve their goals.

The Credit and Investments Ombudsman (CIO) found that James and Carmel were on track to achieve their goals without the gearing strategy that the financial planner provided. It also found that there was no reasonable basis for the advice to establish an SMSF.

The CIO considered that the planner's advice was not appropriate and issued a formal recommendation that the planner pay James and Carmel $141,938 in compensation.

Source: Credit and Investments Ombudsman, 2018

My top ten tips about superannuation

1. Shop around for a low-fee, high-performing fund. Don't just go with a default option. Make a deliberate decision.
2. If your employer has put you into a retail fund – that is, one that's owned by a bank or AMP – it's almost certainly a bad option and you should check the net returns.
3. Long-term returns are what matter.
4. Focus on fees, whatever fund you're in, because fees compound.
5. Every twelve months or so, you should check up on how your fund is going. If they're going badly, you should ask them why, and if you're not satisfied with the answer, you should consider switching funds.
6. Do a budget, and, if you can afford it, top up your super with extra concessional contributions. Tax breaks are hard to come by, and this is one of the few still available.
7. Salary sacrifice is a good way to top up your super.
8. Be very careful about setting up an SMSF, and certainly don't take the advice of someone who stands to benefit from you doing it.
9. Only consider setting up an SMSF if you have more than $300,000 in super. And even then, think twice.
10. Some industry funds offer free financial advice. Take advantage of it.

12

Ethical Investing: Not a Contradiction in Terms

'ETHICAL INVESTING' GOES BY MANY DIFFERENT names, but the principle behind it is simple: investing in a way that minimises harm or maximises social and environmental benefits. Decisions about ethical investing have important implications for investment strategy and investment returns. Apart from selecting ethical stocks, you can invest in an ethical listed investment company (LIC) fund, exchange-traded fund (ETF) or unlisted managed fund. Ethical investments often achieve high returns, because they tend to be run well, and transparently.

Ethical funds can also have high fees due to the additional cost of screening out certain companies and sectors, and identifying highly ethical investments. Ethical investment managers adopt a variety of screening approaches, such as 'positive screening' – whereby the fund manager seeks out companies he or she believes have a positive social or environmental impact – and 'negative screening' – whereby the fund manager avoids companies that have a negative social or environmental impact.

251

Some 'ethical' funds are not very ethical at all: they include shares of companies that engage in demonstrably unethical activities. So, too, some seemingly benign companies engage in activities that are arguably unethical. Woolworths, for example, has Australia's largest poker machine business, with more than 12,000 machines. In 2017, Woolworths reportedly earned $1.2 billion across Australia from poker machines – but you won't see this fact trumpeted in the company's marketing. So if you care about ethics, you need to be wary, and all fund managers should be transparent about what kinds of companies they would invest in. We investors have a right to be well enough informed to make our own judgements about whether or not to participate in a given investment or business activity.

The key point here is that you need to do some of the ethical work. You need to decide your own ethics, then decide how to reflect them in your financial decisions. Ethics are always a personal matter and they require a personal strategy. You can't delegate or contract out your values to someone else.

OTHER LABELS FOR 'ETHICAL INVESTMENT'

- Responsible investment, socially responsible investing and social impact investing
- Sustainable or sustainability investing
- Investing with a social conscience
- Green, eco- or environmental investing (along a spectrum from 'deep green' to 'light green' investments)
- Environmental, social and governance (ESG) investing
- Low carbon investing

Don't be bamboozled by the ever-changing jargon. Many different names are used, but the fundamental principles are the same.

There is a wide range of things that ethical investors avoid: human rights abuses; animal testing and other forms of cruelty; poker machines and other gambling; fossil fuels; carbon pollution; unfair trade; nuclear energy and technologies; landmines and other weapons; harmful chemicals; pornography; the tobacco industry; and other industry sectors that can be harmful to people (including employees), animals and the environment.

Examples of ethical investment funds include Australian Ethical Investment, BetaShares Global Sustainability Leaders ETF, UBS IQ MSCI World (ex-Australia) Ethical ETF, Russell Investments Australian Responsible Investment ETF, Morphic Ethical Equities LIC, and Generation Wholesale Global Share. Most large super funds offer an ethical or sustainable investment option. If you're looking for an ethical investment, I suggest you consider a fund that's a member of the Responsible Investment Association Australasia (RIAA). The RIAA has information on ethical super funds and managed funds.

According to private research reported by David Taylor last year, responsible or ethical investments had more than quadrupled over the preceding three years, to reach approximately $622 billion. *Ethical Investor* magazine and website ranks the environmental, social and governance performance of Australian companies and investment funds. Responsible investment funds have outperformed their mainstream counterparts on several benchmarks. According to the Responsible Investment Benchmark Report 2016, for example, responsible investment Australian equities funds outperformed the ASX 300 and the average large-cap Australian equities funds across one, three, five and ten years.

Some investment managers, such as the Future Generation suite of LICs, take a different approach to ethical investing: they donate 1 per cent of net tangible assets each year to a specified group of charities.

AUSTRALIAN ETHICAL INVESTMENT

Australian Ethical Investments listed in 2002 at 10c a share and six years ago was still just 20c. In June 2019 was trading at $1.78, which means it has produced a phenomenal return of 44 per cent a year since 2013.

Phil Vernon, the managing director, says: 'The company's been going for 30 years. The track record of our Australian Ethical shares fund has been going for over 20 years and it's returned about 10 per cent per annum over that period. [That] is about 3 per cent more than the market that we benchmark against.'

My ethics

I don't like gambling (you've probably already worked that out!) and I will never invest in a gambling business – so Woolworths is out for me, at least for the time being. Nor will I gamble with my money, inside or outside the financial markets.

I believe the science about climate change, and will not invest in activities that will worsen the climate.

I'm not interested in outsourcing my ethics to an ethical investments fund or something similar. I want to make my own decisions about ethics.

There is an important relationship between investment returns and ethics. There is much to be said for maximising your investment returns (in an ethical way) so that you maximise the amount you have available to contribute to charities and other good causes. Economic impact and social impact are not mutually exclusive.

Investment is about earning the greatest return possible. Life is about making the best use of your time and resources.

Louise Walsh, Jenifer Willig and David Fanger are all active in the field of ethical investment, using strategies and philosophies we can learn from.

EXAMPLE 1: LOUISE WALSH

Louise Walsh is CEO of Future Generation, which includes Future Generation Investment Company and Future Generation Global. Each of these is a listed investment company. They are 'funds of funds': the money is managed by other fund managers, somewhere between 15 and 20 fund managers, and they provide their services for free. Future Generation pays 1 per cent of the funds each year to charities.

They choose and list the charities and keep you up to date. If you put in enough money – it has to be quite a lot of money – you get to choose the charity. I think it's a wonderful idea, and it's been going very well. The LICs trade at a big premium to NTA. They've produced decent returns from inception thanks to the skills of the fund managers who actually invest the money, and you not only get a decent return but you are contributing to charity at the same time.

You're contributing to charity without actually costing yourself much money because the returns are decent. I'm a big supporter of Future Generation and I'm an ambassador for one of the charities that they provide money for, which is the Australian Indigenous Education Foundation, which I'm happy to support as it's a wonderful charity.

EXAMPLE 2: JENIFER WILLIG

Jenifer Willig is founder of a social impact consultancy, motive. She's also co-founder of social enterprise WHOLE WORLD Water, with a mission to raise $1 billion a year for clean and safe water initiatives around the world.

Forever changed by her experience as CEO of (RED), the AIDS initiative founded by Bobby Shriver and U2 frontman Bono, Jenifer discovered a passion for driving social change through business. Today she's a social impact entrepreneur whose work has touched thousands of lives and raised millions of dollars.

EXAMPLE 3: DAVID FANGER

David Fanger is the CEO and founder of Swell, an impact investing platform that helps people invest in equity portfolios that map to the UN Sustainable Development Goals. Swell looks at what a company does, not just how they do it.

Leaving a legacy

The next few decades will see a major transfer of wealth from retirees to their children. Many of the recipients of this wealth will be comfortably well off in their own right, prompting more Australians to explore philanthropy. If you're in the lucky position of knowing your family is provided for, you may want to consider leaving part of your estate to charity. There are many ways to do this. The decision depends on the amount of money you have available to give and the level of control you wish to exercise over the distribution. These are the most common approaches:

A one-off bequest to charity

This is the simplest method. Once you have included the correct name of the charity in your will, no further involvement on your part is required. The disadvantages are that you have no control over how the money is spent and you receive no tax benefit in your lifetime.

Setting up a private ancillary fund (PAF)

The first of these tax-deductible private foundations was approved in 2001 and they have quickly become a popular philanthropic vehicle, particularly for people with a lot of money to leave behind. The foundations can be set up to operate in perpetuity or for a fixed term. Gifts made to a PAF can have beneficial tax treatment; check with your accountant. The PAF must abide by specified rules, such as the requirement to distribute a certain proportion of its capital value to charity every year, and the need to have a formal investment plan. Due to their tax treatment, PAFs can be especially attractive for people who have received large, one-off capital gains, an inheritance or a large bonus. Perhaps more importantly, PAFs allow people to see the benefits of giving during their lifetime, and they allow people to involve their children or grandchildren in the giving process. You can download a model trust deed and guidelines from the ATO.

Leaving money in your will to establish a foundation

Philanthropic foundations are essentially a testamentary trust established as part of your will. You can create one with a particular sum of money or specific assets, or the residue of your estate once family members have been allocated a fixed sum. The money can be used to fund a broad range of charities and individuals, and there may be tax benefits for your estate. A foundation may also be used to involve future generations of your family in philanthropy, including the management of the trust itself. The Myer Foundation is probably Australia's best-known example of a charitable foundation.

For more information on charitable giving, visit the websites of Philanthropy Australia and the Australian Charities and Not-for-profits Commission (ACNC).

✓ **Tip:** When selecting a charity, consider how much it spends on administration, including the salaries of its managers. The website of the ACNC has information about charities, including ones that gouge or otherwise misbehave.

KEY POINTS ABOUT ETHICAL INVESTING

1. Invest with high-integrity people.
2. It's your money, so make your own decisions about what is ethical. Don't just invest based on a label or a fad or a clever pitch.
3. Choose your own ethics, then choose your investments and your advisers to suit those ethics.
4. Work with an adviser to decide how you will leave a legacy.

13

Investing into the Future

O NE OF THE THINGS THAT LED ME TO WRITE this book was a special event in 2018: the birth of my first grandchild, Alfie (sort of named after me – or rather my nickname). It made me think about what the future holds for him. What's the world going to be like in 2058, when he's forty and I'm, er, 106? I think about how much the world has changed since I was twenty-six, having just got married, and how the pace of change seems to be accelerating.

It's impossible to tell what the world will be like, of course, as we had no idea in 1978 what it would be like in 2018. Quite often things take longer to happen than you expect and then happen with a rush, a bit like the proverbial bloke who was asked how he went bankrupt. 'Slowly,' he replied. 'And then suddenly.'

I was also motivated by the royal commission, which has felt like both a vindication and a call to action. Having campaigned against the conflicts and corruption in the investment services industries for more than fifteen years, I'm relieved to see it being exposed for all to see and for the regulators to finally do something about it.

I think we are at a turning point. The reason dodgy financial planners, wealth managers and banks were able to take advantage of so many people was that they were given control of the money.

But now, I hope, that tide may be turning. It's time for Australians to take back control. That does not mean investing it yourself, any more than you would operate on your own gall bladder or restump your own house. Taking control means knowing what's going on and being in a position to direct the business of helping you. That's all it is: you're hiring someone to help you do something you can't do for yourself, but that doesn't mean you give up all control of the process.

So this final chapter is in two parts: how I think the world is changing, and how to bring everything you've learnt in this book together into a set of principles you can use and adapt as your life changes.

First, let's look at some megatrends that affect us all in many ways, but especially financially.

Megatrends

'Megatrends' are the sweeping changes and fundamental forces that shape our world and our future. There are times when the megatrends seem more mega than usual, and now seems to be one those times.

Some of this has to do with the aftermath of the second worst global recession in a few generations, but apart from the global problems that are challenging people everywhere, such as refugees, trade wars and climate change, there are some big issues confronting Australians that are homegrown. Many of them come out of Australia's particular brand of politics – which has seen six prime ministers in eleven years (one of them twice) – or at least as it's been practised over the past fifteen years. I'm talking mainly about the energy crisis, the infrastructure deficit resulting from a big increase in immigration, and household debt.

One really good thing to have come out of Australian politics during the past fifteen years has been the free trade agreement with China, which Andrew Robb negotiated during his brief time as trade minister. China continues to grow in importance for Australia and having a formal trade agreement with them (it's not free – free trade agreements are never entirely free) is a very good thing.

And then there's blockchain and artificial intelligence, the two global technology megatrends that Australia is trying hard to keep up with and, surprisingly perhaps, doing okay at.

So those are the megatrends I want to talk about here: transport, energy, infrastructure, debt, China and blockchain/AI. Let's take them one at a time.

Transport

I'm talking about two things here: autonomous cars and drones, although they could perhaps be lumped together: autonomous vehicles, both on the ground and in the air. Together they represent the biggest transport revolution since the internal combustion engine and powered flight.

In some ways, drones seem more ordinary than autonomous cars – after all, we've had model aeroplanes for a long time. But I'll explain why they are possibly a bigger deal.

A book published last year about the race to build driverless cars, called *Autonomy* by Lawrence Burns, started with this paragraph:

> The way we get around is changing. For the first time in 130 years, we're in the midst of a major transformation in automobile transportation. In contrast to the personally owned,

gasoline powered, human-driven vehicles that have dominated the last century, we're transitioning to mobility services based on electric-powered and driverless vehicles, paid
for by trip or through subscriptions.

That scenario still feels rather distant, a bit like science fiction,
although there is definitely a lot of money going into it to make it
happen. I reckon Alfie probably will be ordering a driverless car
with an app on his phone (unless it's a chip buried in his brain
by then).

But I think drones are a whole different kettle of fish, because
of what happened on 4 August 2018. On that day the president
of Venezuela, Nicolás Maduro, was targeted in an assassination
attempt using a drone. The attempt failed, but it highlighted the key
difference between drones and the other big three types of vehicles
that changed the world over the past 200 years: planes, trains and
automobiles. The difference is that drones can carry bombs and
cameras, presenting a whole new set of challenges.

Drone terrorism? Of course. Suicide bombing has its limita-
tions, let's face it. Brainwashing is expensive and time-consuming.
But now you can just nip down to Harvey Norman and pick up
a quadcopter for less than a hundred dollars and rig it up with some
C-4 and a mobile phone detonator and point it at the intended
victim. Far easier than hijacking a whole plane, for example.

And regulation of drones to protect privacy is also going to be
a big deal. I don't just mean the Civil Aviation Safety Authority's
safety rules, which are already extensive – there will have to be a
big set of privacy rules specific to drones as well.

Facial recognition is another modern invention that is changing
the world. Up to now, surveillance has been confined to cameras
attached to walls, but it won't be long before top-of-the-head
recognition is a feature of drone software.

Drones can see over fences, and there will no doubt soon be tiny drones the size of insects, barely visible, with tiny cameras, flying through open windows and into rooms for a peek, and sending the pictures back live to head office, whatever and wherever that might be.

So maintaining both security and privacy in the era of drones, artificial intelligence, GPS navigation, powerful explosives, tiny cameras and facial recognition is going to require industrial-scale regulation and policing. This is a massive task that governments have barely begun to get their heads around.

Not that privacy is an issue confined to drones. When Scott McNealy, the founder of Sun Microsystems, famously declared in 1999 that, 'You have zero privacy ... get over it', nobody really knew what he meant. Now, thanks to Facebook and Google, we definitely know.

The transport revolution is going to present both challenges and opportunities for investors and for society. Lithium, a key material in batteries, is the new oil. Or is it? And if it is, what does the demand/supply balance look like? After all, oil supply is fraught and political, but we understand it well after a century of getting it from the Middle East. Who controls lithium? Not to mention the other ingredients in batteries, like cobalt and graphene.

And while regulating drones and defending against them are going to be big businesses, the main business cases will involve using them – for small freight like pizzas and parcels, perhaps eventually carrying people, and surveillance of things like farm fences, livestock, crowds, houses (for real estate agents, architects and solar panel installers). They are going to be used by every part of society – consumers, businesses and governments of all types, just like planes, trains and automobiles.

And the reason drones may end up being a bigger deal than those other modes of transport is that they are a lot more than mere transport, either of freight or people. They're also flying cameras, flying computers and flying robots. And maybe flying bombs.

Energy

The megatrend with energy is, of course, the global shift from fossil fuels to renewable energy, mainly wind and solar. It is caused by the worldwide effort to deal with climate change, despite the sometimes bitter debate about whether it's real or not, as well as the plummeting cost of photovoltaic solar panels and wind turbines, which is part of the general decline in the price of technology. Over the past decade, Australia has managed to shoot itself in the power point, so to speak, and instead of being an exciting opportunity for investors, energy has been a matter of crisis and a disruptive political argument for a decade.

At the same time as the rest of the world was working towards some kind of scheme to limit carbon emissions a decade ago, Australia lurched into political warfare over it. As a result of the policy vacuum, there was an investment vacuum, so that when two big coal-fired power stations died of old age – Hazelwood in Victoria and Northern in South Australia – supply fell short of demand and prices rose.

It doesn't really matter whether the scientists are right about global warming or are part of a giant left-wing conspiracy, the problem has been the failure to agree on a policy, any policy, coupled with political instability.

But now the global trend towards renewable energy looks unstoppable no matter what politicians do, and it does represent a long-term investment opportunity, as well as a threat to incumbent energy companies, especially those relying on fossil fuel.

One of the most important megatrends is what they call 'behind the meter' generation – that is, power generated by those who are usually just customers of the big energy companies. I'm talking not just about solar panels on the roofs of our houses, although that's becoming a very big deal, but also about industrial users generating their power, such as shopping centres and warehouses. Even Telstra has decided, in effect, to own its own solar power station.

And pretty soon all these households and businesses generating their own power will be able to trade electricity with each other, bypassing the big companies entirely.

Population growth

Since 2005, Australian governments have, in effect, been using population as economic policy.

In a way, it's understandable. Having fully outsourced monetary policy to the Reserve Bank in 1996, and having lost wages policy long ago to enterprise bargaining and control of fiscal policy to ballooning health and welfare costs, which have gobbled up the Budget, there was nothing left: the number of people who are let into the country is about the only economic lever the government directly controls these days.

Net migration used to average about 80,000 a year during the 1970s, 1980s and 1990s, and after 2005 it was reset to 240,000. Births also kicked up from 120,000 a year to between 150,000 and 160,000.

This was the most significant economic policy change since the floating of the dollar, and it has several important consequences, some good, some less so, some unknown, and all of them add up to a megatrend. Even if the migration is reduced again, that decade or so of a tripling of the rate will have a long-term impact on the Australian economy.

More likely, strong population growth, especially in Melbourne and Sydney, will continue to support both house prices and housing construction, in particular high-rise apartments, although both of those things are in a down-cycle at the moment.

But while apartments are easily funded and simple to build, new immigrants buy cars, as well as houses and flats, and roads are more difficult. Some are privately funded, but most need to be paid for by governments, and they're largely out of cash. The result is a megatrend of infrastructure deficit, traffic congestion and falling productivity as a result.

Household debt

This is not a great trend, let's face it, but it's definitely mega. Since the GFC in 2008, global debt has grown from 170 per cent of world GDP to 220 per cent, which equates to about US$170 trillion. Yes, I know, any number with thirteen zeroes, as that one has, starts to lose all meaning, but global debt is about as mega as a trend can get. And Australia is out there near the front of the pack. Australian household debt is 120 per cent of GDP and 190 per cent of income, about the highest in the world on that measure. This is probably the greatest risk facing investors, especially with a declining property market, and to some extent it's due to the previous megatrend on my list: population growth.

Immigration is one of the things that has kept wage growth low, by creating a large pool of labour, along with automation, low productivity growth and the shift in power from labour to companies. Low wage growth, causing low inflation, is keeping interest rates down, and that, in turn, encourages more debt. That's what it's meant to do. Monetary policy acts by encouraging or discouraging borrowing by manipulating interest rates. Interest rates have been at a record low for more than two years. Lots of debt is the inevitable, intended result.

It's not just immigration. Female participation in the workforce is at a record high, and that isn't being caused by a resurgence of feminism. It's because high household debt means both partners have to get a job to pay the mortgage.

That means interest rates will stay where they are for a long time to come, apart from some out-of-cycle increases by banks adjusting for the rise in wholesale funding costs, based on rising US interest rates.

And as the Reserve Bank itself has noted, high debt makes Australian households more vulnerable to shocks.

China

In many ways, China is Australia's most important megatrend, and has been since US president Richard Nixon went there in 1972 to begin the West's engagement with what was then Mao Zedong's closed empire, and it was kicked along when China joined the World Trade Organization in 2001, beginning the biggest resource boom in our history.

Ever since 1972, there has been a kind of 'frenemy' tension playing out between America and China that started with the United States using it to isolate Russia (then the Soviet Union) and has been recently getting ratcheted up by President Donald Trump's trade wars.

Underlying all this is a kind of 'bet' between them, as Dr Sam Wylie of Melbourne Business School put it in a recent essay: 'The US (or more generally the Western alliance) is betting that China cannot build a highly developed economy without becoming a democracy. China (more specifically the governing Communist Party) is betting that it can.'

Australia's money is on China. Mining exports remain by far the nation's main money earner, mainly to China, now being joined by natural gas from northern Queensland, and dairy products, in particular infant formula. And then there's education and tourism, third and fourth biggest export earners, also now dominated by China. This is a megatrend that has a long way to run.

But the relationship with China is complicated, partly because of the growing trade tensions between it and our main ally, America, and also because China uses market access and tourism as a tool of foreign policy.

It's not just Australia. China toys with the world's corporations in three ways: first, it turns market access on and off, apparently on a whim, driving companies to distraction; second, it requires foreign businesses to go into joint ventures over which they have no control and through which their technology is transferred to China; and third, it is using tourism as a weapon.

Unlike Australia's exports of iron ore, which are vital to the Chinese steel industry and can't be stopped, the flow of tourists can be, and is, turned off overnight if a country does something to displease Beijing.

And companies that export discretionary goods to China, as opposed to non-discretionary raw materials, know they are living on a knife's edge, and could lose their licences tomorrow.

China seems to withdraw import licences just to keep its hand in, to show that it can, and to make sure nobody gets too complacent, including Chinese consumers.

The bigger question is whether China can grow into a fully developed economy with high levels of per capita GDP without becoming a democracy. I suspect it can't and that the Chinese Communist Party will have to relinquish its monopoly on power, but the road to getting there could be very rocky indeed.

So although the growth of China into a rich superpower is clearly a positive megatrend for Australia, it's a risky one.

Blockchain and AI

I recently interviewed a bloke named Guy Maine, the managing director of an ASX-listed business called BidEnergy. The company uses robotic process automation (RPA) to check energy bills and organise auctions, so its customers can get the cheapest energy.

Maine and his board are quickly taking the company to the US and the UK. Their aspirations are global, as are those of dozens of listed Aussie start-ups and mid-cap tech companies using AI and blockchain, led by the ASX itself, which is working to move its settlement system onto blockchain.

That's just one small example of what's happening thousands of times around the globe, all the time. A bigger one is that the World Bank has mandated Australia's Commonwealth Bank to create a 'blockchain bond' – that is, a debt security that exists entirely on a blockchain. What does that mean? Well, it's a hard idea to get one's head around but basically it means the security has no paper existence and all information and transactions for it sit on thousands of computers around the world. The 'distributed ledger', as it's called, means that everything is automatically securely verified because it's impossible to change records on so many computers.

It also means the internet is in the early stages of a massive paradigm shift powered by decentralised computing on public blockchains, and it is now a question of when this shift happens, not if.

The internet lowered the barriers for the flow of information globally; smart contract platforms backed by AI and blockchain will create a layer of trust across all digital participants, while greatly improving the efficiency of transactions and the security of data.

The fact that the ASX is preparing to move the CHESS settlement system to distributed ledger technology, or blockchain, has not only emphasised the legitimacy of the paradigm shift but also helped take Australia to somewhere near the forefront of it.

It's perhaps appropriate that I finished this megatrends section with blockchain and AI, because these are the most mysterious elements of our future and the ones with the most potential to change our lives – but in ways we can't yet understand.

As Soren Kierkegaard said: 'Life can only be understood backwards, but it must be lived forwards.'

Predicting the future

That's the trouble with investing – it's all about the future, which we can't know, we can only make a stab at it.

In 2008, the global financial crisis shook our faith in the financial system, and revelations at the Hayne Royal Commission have been doing it again. Now is the time to take more control of your own money and to use prudent but powerful investment strategies. With this book, I want to reassure people that, with a few careful steps and some practical wisdom, you can take control and you can invest safely and successfully, either on your own or employing experts to help you.

The fundamentals of growing a nest egg aren't complicated. They boil down to good housekeeping plus some diligence and a good dose of common sense. Spend less than you earn, invest the difference in the right kind of fund, and let the magic of compound interest do the work for you. As part of that, it's

✓ **Tip:** Never forget the fundamentals – understanding risk, return, preferences and goals. And never forget why you are investing.

really important to understand the difference between investing and speculating. The difference is simple: investing is about using compound interest and/or yield (income); speculating is a game of pass the parcel, where you don't open it.

You should choose a good adviser, fund manager or super fund in the same way you would choose a good carpenter or accountant. They're providing you with a service and there are plenty more where they came from, so it's not only a good idea to shop around and get quotes, it's essential. And with good advice you'll be able to avoid many of the worst pitfalls, while making good use of the tax-effective superannuation system.

Building wealth requires a disciplined approach to investing, where you remain invested and you don't jump in and out of the market trying to time its ups and downs, paying costs every time you do. An old saying in investing is: it's time in the market, not timing the market, that matters.

It's also true that there are times when you should not buy shares, because they are overpriced and are likely to fall. It took twenty-five years for the Dow Jones index in the United States to get back to where it was in September 1929. Those who invested in the Nasdaq in early 2000 waited a long time for their investments to rise back to half the index's peak value.

Discipline can be difficult when your investments are experiencing volatility. This is why it is important to have some understanding, some good advice, and a strategy, including some diversification, so that if some of your investments do take a hit you have another part of your portfolio picking up the slack and giving you some stability. As Warren Buffett said: 'I will tell you how to become rich. Close the doors. Be fearful when others are greedy. Be greedy when others are fearful.'

It is hard to sell out when everyone else is saying that the only way is up. *The Big Short* dramatised this feeling very well. When a hedge fund trader shorted the banks, betting on a financial crisis, some of his investors failed to hold their nerve. They removed their money from the fund – a decision that they would very much regret. When the slump did in fact arrive, the fund earned massive returns.

But trying to time the market on a day-to-day basis with any precision is a mug's game. Short-term price fluctuations are unpredictable and tend to cancel each other out. Some traders and professionals profit from this and may be feted as heroes for a time, but luck plays a large part here. Few people get it right consistently.

This doesn't mean, however, that you should ignore timing altogether. For one thing, some market cycles – such as in the property market – turn slowly, and are therefore fairly easy to pick. The key thing when it comes to the big cycles is to know where you are. Whether you are at a high point or a low one makes a big difference about whether you should buy or sell. As always, expert advice is crucial.

BUYING AND HOLDING AND SHARE MARKET CYCLES

If you invested $10,000 in the Australian share market in June 1970 and left it there until June 2009, it would have been worth $453,165, a return of more than 10 per cent a year. The best single monthly return was 26 per cent, in October 1974. Missing that would have cost you $92,109, and would have reduced the final value of your investment to $361,056. Missing the two best months would have reduced your final balance to $299,950; that's a reduction of 34 per cent. These two best months, October 1974 and January 1975, followed the worst market crash since 1929.

Likewise, investors who sold shares and fled to cash when the market bottomed in early 2009 would have missed the remarkable 50 per cent rebound that followed soon after.

A good rule to live by: When everyone, including politicians and taxi drivers and Uber drivers, is saying that the economic cycle is over, and that we will be in a boom forever, it is time to sell.

The timeless reality is that while progress in science is always onwards and upwards, and today's scientists are always standing on the shoulders of those who came before, markets and economies move in cycles. That's because greed wipes out people's memory of what happened before, and as the saying goes, those who forget history are doomed to repeat it.

Past performance is not a guide to future performance, but often it's all you have to go on. If a fund has consistently outperformed, it is fair to surmise that the fund's managers know what they are doing.

If you want to grow your money, you have to find a fund manager who is good at it. A track record of consistently outperforming is a good indicator of this.

Liquidity, high-performing investments and the future of super

The Future Fund, one of the nation's best performing funds, invests in proportionally few Australian shares. As at 30 June 2018, domestic equity investments make up only 6.7 per cent of its investments, and another 25.5 per cent is in international equities. The rest is in property, infrastructure and timberland, and alternative investments including private equity. The high weighting of alternative investments – many of which are illiquid – is one reason why the Future Fund performs so well, so consistently.

Australia's big super funds have been increasing their investments in private equity and other alternative investments, and this is driving higher returns. (This is important; the stories in the media about rampant private equity investors pillaging companies may seem distant, but they are affecting you directly via your super.)

Super funds have suffered in relative terms, however, by the requirement to maintain a high degree of liquidity, something the Future Fund doesn't have to do. Law requires super funds to be able to give you your money within three days, or at least to let you roll it over into another fund. This rule means funds have to maintain high liquidity just in case, and it's penalising all of us through lower returns on our super. A better solution would be to require a longer notice period – of, say, six months – so that the super funds could have more certainty and greater scope to chase less liquid but better performing investments. There would be a trade-off in terms of less competition, but in my view it's one worth having.

If you elect to set up a self-managed super fund, you can determine your investment horizon and your own level of liquidity. The downside with such funds is that, as discussed, they can be onerous in terms of the time and administration required, and they are probably not worth it if the amount of your super is less than $300,000. Another alternative is to look for more specialised super funds that better suit your plans and your horizon. Some types of industry super funds tend to invest more in illiquid investments. The level of liquidity should be a focus when thinking about which fund to entrust your money to.

As the super market (not the supermarket!) evolves, I'd like to see a more investor-focused offering of retirement income products, and a wider range of choice about investment time frames and liquidity. In a better world, there would be a market-driven menu of choices including high-liquidity, fast-access funds and low-liquidity, slow-access ones. And super funds would see their business as 'providing retirement incomes', not just managing super.

Building the new future of financial advice and integrity

The royal commission highlighted in the starkest possible way the difference between good and bad financial advice. So did the earlier collapse of Westpoint and other debacles.

In this book, I've painted a picture of a better financial future, and a better financial system. But to a large extent, it's in your hands: you can help bring about this better future and this better system by doing the following things:

- forcing planners to compete for your business
- only engaging planners who are experienced and well qualified
- rating the performance of the planners you use and reporting any misconduct
- demanding that all fees and charges be transparent
- only paying for actual services.

There should be, and probably will be, a lot more regulation of financial services to come out of the royal commission, but there's only so much that regulation can do. In the end, it's up to us to make the system better.

Banks and financial advisers have become lazy, and in some cases, corrupt, because we let them. ASIC and APRA were also asleep at the wheel, and to some extent deliberately colluded with the industry to preserve stability and strength at the expense of competition, integrity and putting clients' interests first. In other words, I think the regulators have tended to put the interests of the institutions first, partly because the GFC was such a searing experience for them. The pendulum of regulation swung too far towards the prevention of systemic crisis and away from the protection of the customers.

Now the pendulum is swinging back the other way, and about time too.

A VISION OF THE EMERGING FUTURE

Planners diagnose and treat financial planning problems and prescribe solutions in the same way doctors prescribe medicine – uncorrupted by sales commissions or management directives from drug companies.

Financial advice is more relevant, impartial and cheap. Investors reliably receive good value for money from the financial services sector.

Investors have better choices. The advice industry has more integrity and tougher regulation. A new breed of financial planner is more common: one with specialised education and advanced qualifications, who charges a reasonable fee for the service provided and doesn't skim a percentage off the top forever.

With greater transparency, including performance ratings, it is easier to find a financial planner who has high integrity and who offers good value.

What makes a successful investor?

- You are serious about investing and are eager to learn.
- You keep up to date with high-level trends and developments in markets.
- You know what separates investing from speculating.
- You take responsibility for planning and activating your own investment strategy.
- You know how to be in charge. You retain control of your money, even if you use a professional adviser.
- You aren't mesmerised or overawed by the poster boy fundies and investment icons.
- You know that even the most astute and well-informed

investor can make mistakes. They are often taken by surprise – by market developments, by corporate disruption and by fraud. Warren Buffett admits he made 'big mistakes' in the past by not selling some of his larger holdings when stock prices were higher than the stocks' intrinsic values.

- You rely on science and real evidence, not 'good luck' or 'gut feel'. According to Benjamin Graham, the father of 'value investing', the investor's worst enemy is usually him or herself. Investors often base decisions on shaky foundations: guesses, emotion, fear of loss or regret, fear of missing out, overconfidence, or biased interpretation of evidence. You, in contrast, seek good advice – and you put it into practice.

A few words to end with

I really hope the Hayne Royal Commission, for all its failings, becomes a sort of inflection point, when Australians' attitudes to the financial system changed forever. Before Hayne, there was trust based on ignorance and faith; after Hayne, there's knowledge and, I hope, a steely desire to do something about it – to take back control.

In a way that's never been done before, the royal commission exposed how the financial sector abuses its power and exploits its information, and that's to Kenneth Hayne's and his staff's great credit. They did a fantastic job laying bare the way the industry uses that knowledge gap to take customers to the cleaners – not always, but too often.

So it's time now to do something about it, to take back control. In almost fifty years of analysing this world, I know that it's like the Wizard of Oz behind the curtain – made out to look scary, but when you pull back the curtain, it's just another salesperson trying to sell you something.

So, yes – you can do it!

Useful Sources and Resources

Websites
- ASIC's MoneySmart website: moneysmart.gov.au
- ASIC: asic.gov.au
- ACNC: acnc.gov.au
- Adviser Ratings: adviserratings.com.au
- ASX: asx.com.au
- Association of Financial Advisers: afa.asn.au
- CPA Australia: cpaaustralia.com.au
- Financial Planning Association of Australia: fpa.com.au
- Chartered Accountants Australia and New Zealand: charteredaccountants.com.au
- mybudget.com.au
- investsmart.com.au

Property research sources
- Australian Property Monitors: apm.com.au
- BIS Shrapnel / BIS Oxford Economics: bis.com.au
- Real Estate Institute of Australia: reia.asn.au
- CoreLogic (formerly RP Data): corelogic.com.au
- Residex: residex.com.au

Index

www.ingramcontent.com/pod-product-compliance
Lightning Source LLC
Chambersburg PA
CBHW021551210326
41599CB00010B/404